SUPERFLEX®...
A Superhero Social Thinking® Curriculum

A FUN AND MOTIVATING WAY TO EXPLORE SOCIAL THINKING

By
Stephanie Madrigal, MA, CCC-SLP
&
Michelle Garcia Winner, MA, CCC-SLP

Illustrated by **Kelly Knopp**

Think Social Publishing, Inc.
www.socialthinking.com

Superflex®… A Superhero Social Thinking® Curriculum

Stephanie Madrigal and Michelle Garcia Winner

Library of Congress Control Number: 2007909238

ISBN: 978-0-9792922-4-8

Think Social Publishing, Inc.
404 Saratoga Avenue, Suite 200
Santa Clara, CA 95050
Tel: (408) 557-8595
Fax: (408) 557-8594

This book was printed and bound in the United States by Mighty Color Printing.
TSP is a sole source provider of Social Thinking products in the U.S.
Books may be purchased online at www.socialthinking.com

Dedication

This book is dedicated to my parents, Jimmy and Rosalie Madrigal, who have always inspired and believed in me.

Acknowledgments

Thanks to all the **amazing therapists** at *Michelle G. Winner's Social Thinking Center, Inc.* who have helped to create this concept and our ever-present *Team of Unthinkables*. You have all allowed for the *Superflex*® curriculum to evolve and I thank you for your creativity and excitement with the lessons. Thank you for your daily support. Your words and motivation with the curriculum allowed me to keep pushing forward. **Randi Dodge, Sue Day, Shelly Henderson, Kristi Iwami, Deborah Hoffman, Amy Miller** and **Jaime Rivetts**; you are all amazing and I look forward to many more *Superflex* missions with you. **Cathy Hart**, our office manager and resident counselor for keeping me sane and smiling with her support.

Thanks to the many **families** and **clients** who have helped spark ideas for the lessons, characters and illustrations. I hope that this will provide a useful and fun tool to keep learning about social thinking.

To all the people behind the scenes, professionals who made this idea a reality. Thanks to; **Marilyn Leiker**, my editor and **Beth Blacker**, my graphic designer and to **Kelly Knopp**, my illustrator who, over many long hours, brought my vision of this project to life. Kelly, you are an amazing artist and I thank you for all your help.

Finally, to **my family** who eagerly sat at the dinner table listening to the very first version of my *Superflex* story – what love! You all inspire me on a daily basis. To my two daughters, **Cassandra** and **Rebecca**, who always provided me with unconditional love and hugs during my own *Unthinkable* moments!

Recommended Teaching & Learning Pathway
for using the Superflex Curriculum
3-Step Pathway for ALL kids

1

2

3

Use Social Detective first to introduce key Social Thinking concepts/Vocabulary to build social awareness.

After building social awareness and a social vocabulary, introduce Superflex to teach about self-regulation toward behavior change.

Use any Superflex story books or games AFTER teaching the Superflex Curriculum to take learning on an individual Unthinkable concept to a deeper level.

If you're working with kids ages 9-12

For kids aging out of Superflex (ages 10+)

Start with Social Detective.
Next, Social Thinking and Me is used BEFORE or alongside teaching the Superflex Curriculum.

Start with Social Thinking and Me (if not already taught). Next, move on to Social Fortune or Social Fate. (ages 10+)

Find these and other books and teaching materials at
www.SocialThinking.com

Table of Contents

*Handouts for Rock Brain, Brain Eater, and D.O.F. are embedded in the Lessons, and can be found on pages 33, 59, and 63.

Important Note!

The Superflex curriculum continues to evolve as we adapt and expand these ideas into a better teaching tool that's also culturally sensitive. Over the course of 2021 and 2022, we are updating elements across the curriculum. As part of these updates, we have officially changed the name of the Team of Unthinkables to the **Team of UnthinkaBots**.

To learn more about how you can use the revised UnthinkaBots terminology and introduce the characters that may appear slightly different than in the original curriculum, visit our website: socialthinking.com/SuperflexUpdates

Wait! Don't start using this curriculum until you have considered the below:

Note to parents and professionals:

The purpose of this curriculum and comic book is to provide an engaging teaching tool to help students learn more about their own social behavior and strategies on how to regulate it. The next few pages will give you an introduction to the critical characters (*Superflex*® and *the Team of Unthinkables/UnthinkaBots*) as well as lessons and worksheets for teaching. Additionally, we've included a brief overview for a series of terms/concepts called **Social Thinking®** **Vocabulary**. This vocabulary is considered to be the framework for teaching the *Superflex* lessons. If you are not familiar with how to teach these concepts, please teach the **Social Thinking Vocabulary** concepts with your students. They are taught through the comic book: *You are a Social Detective,* 2nd Edition (Winner & Crooke, 2020) and more comprehensively in *Think Social! A Social Thinking® Curriculum for School Age Students* (Winner, 2005). These resources can be found at our website **www.socialthinking.com**.

It will also be important to pre-teach children that managing an *UnthinkaBle/UnthinkaBot* is something that happens in their brain and not a battle with their bodies.

It is also helpful to note that the *Superflex* curriculum is best suited for those children who are able to differentiate fantasy from reality. This curriculum is for students who can imagine they have *Superflex* within them and will use the strategies in the curriculum to access their own superflexible powers. This is a very different concept than pretending to be a superhero in play.

The Story of Superflex...

The creation of Superflex® was the result of many sessions spent trying to help my students understand the concept of flexible thinking. Many of our students are rigid in their thinking and have trouble shifting their thoughts or plans around the plans of others to adapt to the social world around them. This ultimately makes being a part of a group that much more challenging. In an attempt to relate to my students I thought, "What would really motivate my students to explore this concept?" Then it hit me. . . Superheroes! We all can relate on some level to fantasizing or imagining what it would be like to be a superhero or how much fun it might be to have super powers. Our kids in particular have an amazing sense of imagination and creativity, and I had a feeling they would just run with this idea.

So I took this idea to several of my groups. I explained to my students that as social beings, we are like superheroes in that we are always trying to use our "brain" powers to be flexible thinkers. By thinking about others and what they might need from us, we have the ability to shift and change our thinking at any time to keep others feeling good. However, we are always challenged by our "not-so-flexible thinking" and wanting to do simply what we want to do, when we want to do it. This "not-so-flexible" thinking ultimately becomes our nemesis because we constantly have to regulate and adjust around others even when one does not want to; hence, Social Thinking®. My students quickly and eagerly wanted to give this nemesis a name and discuss all the moments they witnessed "not-so-flexible thinking" occurring in their day.

Eventually we opted to name this character Rock Brain. Rock Brain is the character that gets into our brain and misguides us into thinking only about what we want to do and not be able to see things from someone else's perspective; Rock Brain simply does not allow our brains to shift and adjust to the social world around us. My students were enamored by the idea that they could be superheroes and devise strategies to defeat Rock Brain. They immediately began identifying moments when others were losing the battle to Rock Brain. For even some of my more challenging students who were resistant to working on skills in the group, this became a way for them to remove themselves from the equation of social thinking and allow them to work on these skills in third person. More often than not, these instances included a parent, teacher or classmate at school who was not able to defeat this character. The fact that they could not see themselves struggling with flexible thinking told me I had a lot of work to do.

At the end-of-the-year retreat with my colleagues, I eagerly shared this Superflex idea and the various concepts and lessons that were created, as well as the children's increased motivation and self awareness observed in the sessions. We then found a way to build on the idea of Superflex and use this character to help our students not only increase their awareness of social behaviors like flexible thinking, but also the other social skills that our students have difficulty with, such as keeping their body with the group, attending to the group with their brain, staying on topic, etc. We found a villainous name for each of these behaviors and the Team of Unthinkables () were born!

10

The educators and students at our clinic continue to transform and add to the Superflex idea as a way to help our students understand more about perspective, flexible thinking, problem solving, and how to change their own thinking and behavior. The activities and ways to spin this idea seem endless, and I hope that this curriculum will provide you with some new and fun ways to tackle social thinking with your child or client.

Purpose and goal of the curriculum

The purpose of this Superhero Social Thinking® curriculum (SST) is to provide the Social Thinking educator, teacher, or parent with a fun, motivating, and non-threatening way for our students to explore Social Thinking concepts while increasing their knowledge of social expectations, their awareness of their own behavior and how to modify their behaviors with superflexible strategies.

Our students have difficulty monitoring and regulating their own behaviors in the moment, and this curriculum provides a fun forum in which they can explore their own challenges and identify ways to modify their thoughts and related behaviors in different settings. For many of my students, this has become a very empowering way to help them help themselves.

Good social skills can be defined as "adapting efficiently in each context," meaning we have to read the hidden social rules in each context and then regulate our physical presence, eyes, language, emotions, reactions, etc. This requires highly flexible thinking. While some children learn to do this somewhat effortlessly, our students have challenges in recognizing and applying these concepts to demonstrate social cooperation. When we can incorporate all this information and regulate the body and mind to show we are effectively adapting to others across environmental contexts, we demonstrate that we are considering the perspectives of people across environments. We call this "social smarts."

Students who do not learn this information intuitively, but who function with emerging meta-cognitive language, need to be taught these core concepts more explicitly. Thus, we have developed a superhero named "Superflex" and the "Team of Unthinkables" to contrast for students when we are using our "social smarts" (e.g., using our internal Superflex powers)versus when our brains are getting sidetracked in a less social way, the dominant thinking of a less flexible member(s) of the Team Of Unthinkables. The kids will enjoy the idea that they are superheroes in training and that they are trying to increase their social skills and superflexible thinking to become the Ultimate Superhero! The cast of characters that represent Superflex and our Team of Unthinkables in this curriculum include:

11

Think Social Publishing, Inc. ©2008 www.socialthinking.com

Superhero

Superflex®

Superflex's strengths

Superflex®

Our hero! Totally flexible, trying to figure out people's wants and needs to keep other people calm while also getting his turn to play and to speak as well. He is a great problem solver and can think of many different solutions to one problem.

(Note: in our storybook and curriculum, the Superflex you read about is Aiden's Superflex. Your Superflex looks like you, mine looks like me, etc. Find a fun Superflex is Me handout at the end of the book to draw your own Superflex!)

Team of Unthinkables

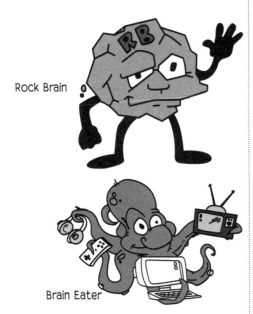

Rock Brain

Brain Eater

Body Snatcher

The "Powers" that the character has over our brains

Rock Brain

Will get the person to do only what he has decided he will do; he will not negotiate with other people. He is not a good problem solver and tries one solution that's not working over and over again. This person may be very rule-bound and rigid in his thinking, seeing only one way to a situation.

Brain Eater

He makes it hard for the person to focus on what he is doing or focus on others during interactions (roll his brain away). Easily distracted!

Body Snatcher

Gets the person to wander off (roll his body away) and not stay with the group or person he is with. May also get the person to turn his body away from the group, not realizing the message he is sending to others.

12

D.O.F. The Destroyer of Fun

This character often pops up during games or activities involving competition. The person becomes overly competitive and insists on going first, playing only what he wants to play and not thinking about compromising and considering another's perspective.

Un-Wonderer

Can prevent the person from showing interest (social wondering) in others or considering what others may want to do based on their interests.

Space Invader

This character makes the person's body move into other people's personal space, not realizing how uncomfortable this makes others feel.

Glassman

Lets a person be flexible to some extent, but then, all of a sudden he just breaks. He doesn't melt down slowly, he quickly starts getting very upset. Glassman usually thinks things aren't "fair."

Grump Grumpaniny

Makes the person think the worst or feel like people are always unkind. He ends up believing it even when people are trying to be nice.

Topic Twistermeister

This character gets the person to twist the topic around and go off on tangents when talking to others. This person may then go on and on about topics that he or she wants to talk about, not realizing that others may be bored or disinterested in what he or she is.

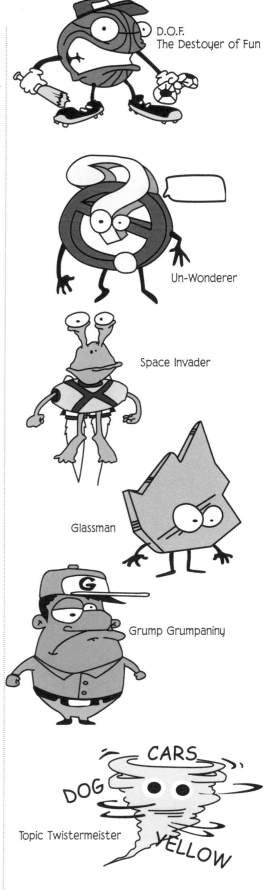

D.O.F.
The Destroyer of Fun

Un-Wonderer

Space Invader

Glassman

Grump Grumpaniny

Topic Twistermeister

13

Think Social Publishing, Inc. ©2008 www.socialthinking.com

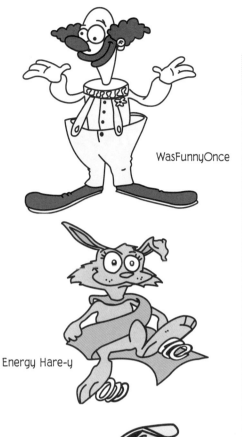

WasFunnyOnce

WasFunnyOnce

This person will attempt to use a lot of humor to be funny. However, he or she does not realize that humor wears out pretty quickly or at times is not funny at all. He or she has trouble recognizing appropriate times for humor and may try to be funny during a discussion in a classroom or when the moment is serious and not funny or silly. For some people, they may get so silly that the other children become silly also, making the group fall apart. This is called getting caught up in the "silly tornado."

Energy Hare-y

Energy Hare-y

This character gives the person so much energy that he is constantly fidgeting or moving around, and he doesn't think about what the people around him need or how others around him are feeling. Sometimes, Energy Hare-y and WasFunnyOnce work together, which can quickly make the group fall apart.

One-Sided Sid

One-Sided Sid

This character gets the person to talk about his own set of topics. Even when someone else brings up his or her interests, he just talks about what interests him. He only thinks about himself and his own thoughts and feelings when he is around others.

Worry Wall

Worry Wall

Makes the person worry so much about the people around him or social situations that he or she "hits a wall" and stops being able to talk at all to the people nearby.

Mean Jean/Gene

Mean Jean/Gene

This person becomes just plain mean to other people. He or she insults or criticizes others. He or she may take things away from them, be very bossy or hog all the attention when others are trying to talk.

14

Think Social Publishing, Inc. ©2008 www.socialthinking.com

*I*n our years at the ***Michelle G. Winner's Center For Social Thinking Inc.***, working with students with social cognitive deficits, we have developed an elaborate list of Social Thinking Vocabulary terms that have made "social" more explicit by providing a language and a way of exploring social information at a deeper level and across all environments. These terms provide a concrete way for our students to explore social expectations when sharing space with others. Some of these terms include thinking with your eyes, rolling your body away from the group, and expected and unexpected behaviors. The Social Thinking Vocabulary also allows for our students' caregivers to understand what is introduced in the groups and reinforce these skills outside of the clinic. All caregivers working with our students would benefit from learning and using the concepts that are introduced. What the educator will quickly find is that these concepts can easily be used with many students in the classroom who are devoid of a social cognitive diagnosis. *Think Social! A Social Thinking®* *Curriculum for School-Age Students* (Winner, 2005) provides a plethora of lessons to help students learn a wide range of the Social Thinking Vocabulary and related methodology concepts. Crooke, Hendrix and Rachman (2007) demonstrated the efficacy of using Social Thinking Methodology vocabulary and related concepts to help promote social learning and generalization of concepts beyond the therapy room.

The SST curriculum was created by elaborating on the concept of "flexible thinking" and diving into a new and deeper way to explore its social concepts. Many of the Social Thinking Vocabulary terms are embedded in the lessons in this book. Each lesson will provide a review of the concept and/or vocabulary terms used within the lesson; however, for a deeper understanding of the concepts or to provide specific lessons on a concept, they are described in greater detail in Michelle G. Winner's books, (2000, 2002, 2004, and 2005). Below is a list of the Social Thinking Vocabulary terms that are embedded within the SST curriculum, virtually all of these concepts are introduced in further detail in the book, *Think Social!* (Winner 2005). The SST curriculum will best be utilized only after clinicians/teachers have a solid foundation in the Social Thinking Methodology reviewed in, *Thinking About You, Thinking About Me,* 2nd Edition (Winner 2007) and *Think Social!* (Winner, 2005).

Social Thinking Vocabulary (*Think Social!, 2005*)

Flexible thinking (Superflexible thinking): Mental flexibility of your brain to interpret verbal and non-verbal information based on different points of view or different contexts. This is the opposite of having a Rigid Brain (Rock Brain) where one follows a rule all the time or cannot interpret subtle different meanings in language or expression.

Keeping your body and brain in the group: Understanding that our bodies need to look interested and connected to the group and our brain needs to keep thinking about what the group is thinking in order to participate in the group. We also teach that people can see when your body or brain does not appear to be a part of the group.

Your body rolled out of the group: A student's body is turned or physically moved away from the group, and the others notice that the student is not working as part of the group.

Your brain rolled out of the group: A student's brain is distracted from what the group is doing and the other people in the group notice that he does not appear to be working as part of the group, even if his body is in the group.

Blue thoughts (good), red thoughts (not so good/weird thoughts): Refer to how our actions, words and even physical dress or hygiene create good thoughts and weird thoughts in other's brains (i.e., the impressions that we make). All people create good thoughts and weird thoughts across a day. People remember the thoughts they have, but if the student primarily implants good thoughts in people's minds then that is what they think of him or her overall. If a person plants a majority of weird thoughts, then that is what people remember most. Behaving really well after producing a lot of weird thought behaviors still leaves people remembering the weird thoughts.

Thinking about others: Idea that we are constantly considering what others are thinking and feeling in order to monitor and modify our behavior to keep people feeling good.

Whole Body Listening: Idea that the whole body (eyes, ears, mouth, hands, feet, bottom, and brain) needs to be focused on the group in order to listen and to show you are listening.

Following hidden rules: This is to explain that not all rules are clearly announced. Most rules in our world are rules people figure out through observation and experience. If you are not sure of the rules, you can ask someone. For example, a hidden rule of being at school is that you are usually supposed to leave your shoes on, even if you take them off at home.

Doing what is "expected": Understanding a range of hidden rules in every situation; we have to figure out what those rules are and then follow them in order to keep other people feeling good about us.

Doing what is "unexpected": Failing to follow the set of rules, hidden or stated, in the environment.

Social Smarts: Having the ability to read the hidden social rules in each context and the emotions and thoughts of others in order to regulate our physical presence, eyes, language, emotions, reactions, etc.

Science Smarts: Having the ability to easily understand more factually based information. These skills alone make it very challenging to negotiate within the social world because of its abstract nature.

Superflex®: A Superhero Social Thinking Curriculum

Make a "smart guess": Taking information you already know or have been taught and making an educated guess with the information.

A "wacky guess": Making a guess when you have absolutely no information to help you figure out what the guess should be. In school we rarely ask for this type of guess-making, unless students are playing a game.

People-Files: Visual way to help our kids to understand that we all are continually learning information about others and filing it in an organized way in our brain, to recall it later when we see that person again.

Figuring out other people's plans: Determining what people are planning to do next based on their physical actions. We can also start to figure out what people are planning to do by interpreting their movement or eye direction (thinking with your eyes). One must also figure out the subtle meaning within spoken language; this is a higher-level skill.

Social Fake: Demonstrate interest in someone else's topic that he or she does not find inherently fascinating by looking interested and adding his or her thoughts to the conversation.

Boring Moment: A set of socially acceptable behaviors that one uses when he is not interested in what the group is doing at that moment.

Whopping Topic Change: When a comment is made and the listener cannot determine the thread of information that connects this comment to what was previously said, thereby providing a response that is off topic or so far removed from the main concept that it is off topic.

Tiny problem Vs. Big (earthquake) problem: Understanding that problems differ in severity, which then assists in helping one to react appropriately to personal situations.

The Rules Change With Age: Teaching students that the rules they are taught across their childhood change, so they must undo some of the lessons taught to them as they age. Some example of rules students should do when they are 8 years old, but should not do in at school when they are 15 years old include:

- Apologizing by just saying, "I am sorry"; by 15 years old you have to show you are sorry through your actions.

- Hugging your parents when they pick you up at school; by 15 years old you should just acknowledge them by looking at them and saying "hi" in a quiet voice.

Superflex®: A Superhero Social Thinking Curriculum   Think Social Publishing, Inc. ©2008 www.socialthinking.com

Cognitive Behavioral Treatment

There is growing research to support the positive effects of Cognitive Behavioral Therapy (CBT) for students presenting with social-cognitive challenges (Attwood 2006). CBT shares three fundamental propositions: 1. Cognitive activity affects behavior; 2. Cognitive activity may be monitored and altered; and 3. Desired behavior change may be affected through cognitive change (Dobson and Dozois 2001). Cognitive behavioral therapy has been helpful in providing clients with a way to change how they may think and respond to others. Winner, in her article to be published in 2007, comments on the spectrum of educators who have utilized and found value in using strategies that follow a CBT approach with their students that allow students to be "taught more about how their brain works, what information needs to be thought about and how to regulate one's own internal thoughts and external behaviors to help them function more successfully in their own environments." Examples of CBT treatment strategies developed by educators and widely applied across higher-level students with social learning challenges include Social Stories® (Gray 1996), Comic Strip Conversations (Gray 1994), the Incredible 5 Point Scale (Dunn and Curtis 2003) and Social Behavior Mapping (Winner 2007).

The SST curriculum grounds itself in the theory and methodology within a cognitive behavioral framework as it provides an avenue from which the students can begin to explore "thinking" and how to modify their thinking, emotions and actions based on the social context. SST has developed from the core Social Thinking Methodology and strategies introduced in the book, *Thinking About You Thinking About Me*, 2nd Edition (Winner, 2007).

Evidence-Based Practices

Evidence-based practices are generally thought to be clinical practices applied only when there is strong scientific evidence to support their use. However, this is only one of many different definitions of Evidence-Based Practice.

According to the American Speech Language and Hearing Association, ASHA, (2005), evidence-based practices need to consider not only what is the BEST evidence available, but also the level of clinical expertise needed to apply or develop new treatments, along with strong consideration of family and client input.

In this very new treatment area of helping the student with social learning challenges develop social thinking and related social skills, relatively little research-driven evidence is available; however, research indicates that cognitive behavioral techniques, such as those offered by teaching "Superflex," look promising for helping our students. This technique was developed at **Michelle G. Winner's Center for Social Thinking**, which is known internationally as a center devoted to pioneering new clinical treatments for students with social learning challenges (HFA, AS, NLD, ADHD, etc.).

Along with this program being developed by experienced clinicians, parent and client input have been sought and valued throughout the formation of these concepts. As part of our clinic's treatment model, we meet with the parents the final 10 minutes of each session. Parent response to their children learning the concept of Superflex and the Team of Unthinkables has been very positive.

In the spirit of evidence-based practices, Superflex fits into one that is developed from research, clinical expertise and family input. It is also based on the literature of child development and on behavioral teachings.

The SST curriculum is designed to be used with school children, ages 5-10, however how it is used will differ. With students ages 5-7 we teach about Superflex and the Unthinkables, about awareness and identification of the characters. With children this young we don't yet teach strategies nor expect these students to be self-regulating by using them. All lessons in the curriculum, including teaching students strategies to use to defeat their Unthinkables, is appropriate for ages 8-10.

Ages and Population

Some middle school groups have also embraced Superflex. This will be dependent on the maturity and interest level of the students that are being taught. The curriculum can easily be modified to accommodate older students but, again, would be on a case-by-case basis.

This SST curriculum was developed for use with students who are on the higher end of the autism spectrum (HFA, PDD-NOS, Asperger Syndrome), NLD, ADHD, and other related diagnoses. To access the concepts in this curriculum, the students must have expressive language skills, a verbal IQ of about 70 or higher and the ability to begin to think about thinking, which is the emergence of meta-cognition. However, given that most children can relate to superheroes and require some redirection or reminders about social thought and nuances, the typically developing child would benefit as well from the SST curriculum.

Some things to think about before getting started...

When introducing the SST curriculum it is important to clearly make the distinction that these characters are fictional, particularly for those students who have difficulty differentiating reality from fantasy. I will often explain that these characters are pretend and are not really in our brains. This sounds obvious; however, some children immediately assume these characters really exist in their brains, and the characters are actively plotting their next social mistake.

It's very important that students also learn and understand that the Superflex they read about in our comics is Aiden's Superflex and that in this curriculum students are learning to develop their own Superflex powers. Their Superflex

Think Social Publishing, Inc. ©2008 www.socialthinking.com

Superflex is ME!

Here are 3 things I can do well with my superflexible thinking:
1. _____
2. _____
3. _____
97

represents them and their emerging superflexible powers. This means it is described as their own name plus "Superflex" (e.g., Kira's Superflex, Max's Superflex) and each student's Superflex looks like that student (their ethnicity, gender, body shape, size, and pictured with any special devices they use, such as vision glasses, hearing aids, a wheelchair, etc.)

When teaching from our Superflex curriculum, be sure the students in your group each have a picture of their own personally named Superflex - most of them look nothing like Aiden! However, when Aiden/Superflex is the teacher at the Superflex Academy, he then is the wise professor helping students develop their own superflexible powers.

Find a **Superflex is Me** coloring page in the handouts at the end of the book so students can create themselves as Superflex.

It will also be important to stress that the Unthinkable characters are NOT EVIL VILLAINS, which implies that, if a child is working on defeating these Unthinkables, then there is something wrong or evil about them. A core theme throughout the SST curriculum is that we are all faced with our team of Unthinkables, and we each need to learn strategies to minimize the power of the Team of Unthinkables. It is also fair to mention that others have an easier time detecting and defeating their own Team of Unthinkables, which is a main reason that they are working with you.

The SST curriculum has provided a generous list of Unthinkable characters; however, do not hesitate to create even more characters and build upon the lessons provided. Many of the ideas for this curriculum have originated from direct student input, and they love being a part of this program development. Enjoy exploring these concepts with your students and using this information as a launching pad for adding to your Team of Unthinkables and new ways for Superflex to win his battle over all social challenges!

Within the SST Curriculum, specific lessons have been dedicated to the three most prominent Unthinkables (Rock Brain, Brain Eater and D.O.F. The Destroyer of Fun) that frequently make their way into the treatment room. The educators will need to determine, based on the students they are working with and their individual needs, which additional Unthinkable characters will need to be specifically explored. A handout has been developed to introduce each Unthinkable. (See Appendix E. Handouts for Rock Brain, Brain Eater, and D.O.F. are embedded in the Lessons, and can be found on pages 33, 59, and 63.)

Each lesson is accompanied by a handout and Funwork page. Please use your best judgment in modifying the handouts to match the ages and challenges of each child. For example if a child has poor fine-motor skills or is too young to write, allow him or her to draw the answer, or dictate, or describe the answer aloud.

Superflex®: A Superhero Social Thinking Curriculum
Think Social Publishing, Inc. ©2008 www.socialthinking.com

*T*his SST curriculum is divided into three levels:

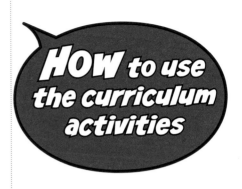

Lessons 1-5 explore the Social Thinking Methodology concepts and vocabulary related to Superflex and the Team of Unthinkables.

Lessons 6-9 increase awareness of the child's own social behaviors he or she is modifying and appropriate strategies.

Lessons 10-13 address self-monitoring and modifying behavior through use of Superflex Strategies.

The following activities are presented in the order we generally introduce them. However, given the individuality among our students, do not hesitate to introduce a lesson that you feel is most appropriate at that moment, with your students. Again, depending on your students, the educator may need to spend additional time exploring additional Unthinkables or various Social Thinking Methodology concepts or vocabulary that are necessary for the child to better understand information being taught in a lesson.

Each lesson should begin with the children donning their capes and grabbing a flexible brain before sitting down at the table. However, given that each child is different, some students may not feel comfortable or feel embarrassed about wearing a cape. A child should not be pressured to put the cape on to be a participant; this is a tiny problem. The cape can be slung on a chair or hung on the wall if the child agrees.

Ideally, the lessons should end with each student receiving a Superflex Award that recognizes their great work for the day. These awards can be posted in the treatment room, or they can be taken home. Groups could even work together to earn enough awards to get a Superhero Party.

Each lesson has an accompanying handout to use in the session and a Funwork assignment that reinforces the concept and provides the parents with an understanding of the information introduced on that day. It is important to provide a weekly Funwork assignment as a way to ensure that the families are learning about the information, concepts, and vocabulary introduced in the treatment sessions. Given that the educator may only spend 30-60 minutes a week with the students, their caregivers become a crucial element to the child's success and progress.

Do not panic! Some lessons may extend over a number of sessions; given the nature of what we are teaching, we can't anticipate the "teachable moments" when we have to stop and work on a specific concept. Do not get discouraged; the lessons will be there when the group is ready to return to the curriculum.

Superflex®: A Superhero Social Thinking Curriculum

Think Social Publishing, Inc. ©2008 www.socialthinking.com

**Lesson #1
The training begins!
How Superflex came to be...**

Purpose: This initial lesson begins the journey of learning about our Social Thinking superhero, Superflex®, while attending sessions each week at the Superflex Academy! Concepts such as **Superflexible thinking***, Rock Brain thinking and Superflexible strategies will be introduced as students read the story *Superflex Takes On Rock Brain and The Team Of Unthinkables. . .A New Beginning*. The students will begin to identify **unexpected behaviors*** that are represented by the Unthinkables.

Vocabulary:

Superflex, **Superflexible thinking***
Team of Unthinkables
Rock Brain, Rock Brain thinking
Superflexible strategy
Expected and Unexpected behaviors*
Thinking with your eyes and brain*
Thinking about others*
Hidden Rules*

Materials:

Story: Superflex Takes On Rock Brain and The Team of Unthinkables-A New Beginning

Capes

Foam brain - small brain replica made out of foam
(ideally one for each student)

Superflex Training Academy Door Sign (see pg. 28)

Handout, Lesson #1

Parent Letter (pg. 27)

Funwork, Lesson #1

Children's books (recommendations in Appendix A)

Definitions-Superflex and Team of Unthinkables Cards (Appendix B)

Superflex Awards (Appendix C)

Goals:

☆ The student will be able to define and identify two examples of "Superflexible" and "Rock Brain" thinking in stories with ___ accuracy in the structured setting.

☆ The student will be able to indicate how others in a story are feeling based on another's "Superflexible behaviors" or "Rock Brain" behaviors with ___ accuracy in the structured setting.

☆ In a drawing, the student will be able to provide two examples of Superflexible thinking (**expected***) with ___ accuracy in a structured setting.

What you need to do before the lesson:

✓ Prior to the children starting their session, place the Superflex Training Academy sign on the door.

✓ Put out capes and flexible brains.

Teacher Review-Superflex Training Session #1

1. When they arrive, tell the children that they will be learning about a Social Thinking Superhero named Superflex. Explain that they are about to enter training at the academy to learn more about this superhero and where they will learn skills to become Superflex themselves!

2. When they enter the room, provide them with a cape and a flexible brain. Ask them to put on their capes and hold on to their flexible brains.

   a. **For some children who are highly distracted, they may use the brain as a fidget during the story, or it may be decided that the cape and brain can be donned at the end of the story.

*Refer to pages 15-17 for definition.

22

Lesson 1: The training begins! How Superflex came to be...

Superflex®: A Superhero Social Thinking Curriculum
Think Social Publishing, Inc. ©2008 www.socialthinking.com

3. Read, *Superflex Takes on Rock Brain and the Team of Unthinkables. . .A New Beginning*.   The story will introduce Superflex, his sidekick Bark and his social ENEMIES, the Team of Unthinkables that are plotting to take over Social Town. (Note: Superflex in this storybook represents Aiden's Superflex.)
   a. During the story, some topics of discussion can be:
      i. What Social Town and its citizens were like before the Unthinkables started taking over.
      ii. **What is expected*** or what are some **hidden rules*** that we have to follow in our society?
      iii. **Flexible thinking*** and why this is important when you are around others. How does **flexible thinking*** show that you are **thinking about others***?
      iv. How was Aiden's mom feeling when he would have Rock Brain thinking? When he was being Superflexible?
      v. How was the neighbor's mom feeling when her son refused to do his homework?
      vi. Encourage discussion of what Unthinkables they notice in themselves and in others.

   It will also be important for the educator to identify which Unthinkable(s) is on their team to demonstrate that this is a challenge we all have to address on some level.

4. Explain to the children that they will have the opportunity to be their own Superflex and their training starts today at the Superflex Training Academy. At the academy, they will learn about some of the most notorious Unthinkable characters that get into our brains, what Unthinkable members are on their team and how to develop their Superflexible strategies to defeat these Unthinkables and become their own ultimate Superhero, Superflex!

5. Explain that all of us have a team of Unthinkables in our brains; some people, however, use their Superflexible strategies and defeat their Unthinkables. Discuss how your students have a harder time with noticing their Unthinkables and calling on Superflex to defeat them. They have to think and work a little harder than some, and that is what they are here to learn. So let's get started!

6. Explain to the students that the hardest part about defeating these Unthinkables is that they are not always obvious and can be very sneaky with their plots to defeat the Superflex in their brain. So they will practice thinking with their eyes and brains to look for clues to spot one of the most notorious Unthinkables, Rock Brain. Have the children each select and read a book, looking to see if they can spot Rock Brain lurking in the pages.

   This activity can also be done with comic strips from the newspaper or video clips from cartoons.

*Refer to pages 15-17 for definition.

23

Lesson 1: The training begins! How Superflex came to be...

Superflex®: A Superhero Social Thinking Curriculum
Think Social Publishing, Inc. ©2008 www.socialthinking.com

7. Pass out Handout Lesson #1, Spot the Unthinkable, and have the children either write or draw:
   a. About the Unthinkable character they found in the story and what the Unthinkable was getting the character to do.
   b. Who won the battle in the character's brain? Superflex or the Unthinkable?
   c. What Superflexible Strategy was used?
8. Have the children share their story and handout with the group.
9. Prior to the session ending, introduce the Superflex awards that will be given each session to those that have demonstrated **Superflexible thinking***. On the award make a note about a positive skill that you observed with each group member (e.g., Johnny, great job **thinking with your eyes*** and spotting the Unthinkable today, or, Johnny was a Superflexible thinker today when he let someone else have the book he wanted, etc.). The children can take these awards home, or they can be displayed in the treatment room for the other students to see.
10. Review Funwork, Lesson 1 with the students.

Funwork, Lesson #1:

The children will be responsible for either writing about or drawing a picture of Social Town and what it would look like if the Unthinkables were all defeated! Ask them to bring back the homework the following week to share with their other Superhero classmates.

The following handouts should also be passed out to parents on the first week:

Parent letter
Definitions: Superflex and Team of Unthinkables Cards
(Appendix B)

*Refer to pages 15-17 for definition.

24

Lesson 1: The training begins! How Superflex came to be...

Superflex®: A Superhero Social Thinking Curriculum
Think Social Publishing, Inc. ©2008 www.socialthinking.com

Spot the Unthinkable®, Rock Brain

How are your *Superflexible senses*? Can you spot an **Unthinkable** when you see one? Well, let's put your brain to the test. Pick a story to read and see if you can spot *Rock Brain* lurking in the story. Draw a picture or write about what your *Superflexible* brain and eyes found.

Title of the book: _____

> Draw a picture or write about what the **Unthinkable** made the character in the story do.

Did *Superflex*® come to the rescue??   ❏ **Yes**   **or**   ❏ **No**

> Draw a picture or write about how *Superflex* defeated *Rock Brain*. What strategy did he use? Or what happened because *Superflex* could not defeat *Rock Brain*?

How did you do at spotting *Rock Brain*?   ❏ **Great**   ❏ **So-So**   ❏ **Needed some help**

Superflex®: A Superhero Social Thinking Curriculum
Think Social Publishing, Inc. ©2008 www.socialthinking.com

Cleaning up Social Town...

The **Unthinkables**® have all been defeated!!! Create a picture of what *Social Town* would look like now. Draw three examples of citizens using their *Superflexible* thinking and thinking about others. **Ahhhh... What a great place to live.**

Hey! don't forget to put **Superflex**® in your picture somewhere. Without Superflex, there would be no *Social Town!*

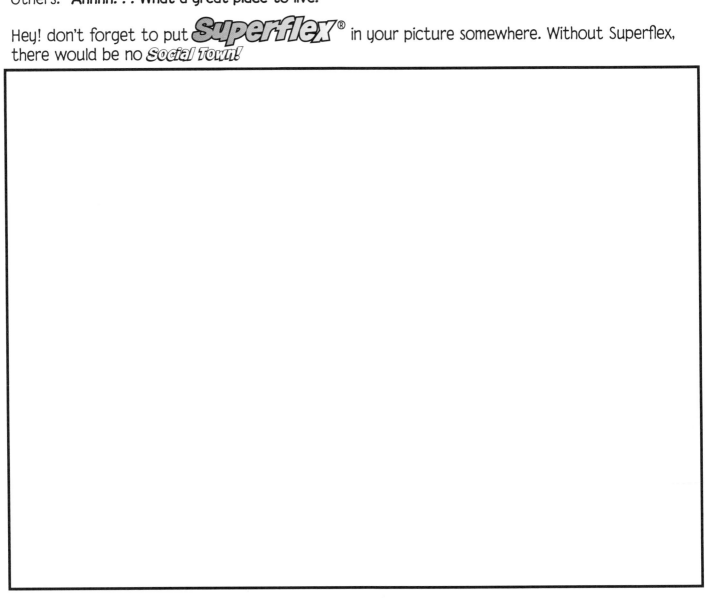

Did you notice any *Rock Brain* moments happening in your town? Describe or draw below.

26

Lesson 1: The training begins! How Superflex came to be...

Superflex®: A Superhero Social Thinking Curriculum
Think Social Publishing, Inc. ©2008 www.socialthinking.com

Superflex® — Our Social Thinking® Superhero!

Dear parents and educators,

The children are continuing to learn about the Social Thinking Methodology through the use of a fun, new curriculum using a social-thinking superhero named **Superflex!** This curriculum is used with our elementary and younger middle school students.

The goal of this curriculum is to provide a fun, motivating way to improve the child's social and behavioral flexibility and to ultimately develop better self-monitoring and self-feedback loops for their social behavior. The concept is based on the ideas that we all have a superhero, **Superflex**, in our brains, who is constantly battling the **"Team of Unthinkables"** (a variety of unexpected behaviors) such as: the **Un-Wonderer, Space Invader, and Brain Eater, etc.,** who may come and try to take over our brains. The students will be able to identify what members are on their **Team of Unthinkables** and learn **Superflexible Strategies** to defeat their **Unthinkables®** when they challenge **Superflex.**

The lessons will progress through and provide several opportunities for the child to learn about various **Unthinkable** characters while building on his or her ability to recognize these behaviors in themselves and others, and using the **Superflexible Strategies** to modify their behavior. Every child has a **Superflex** inside!

It will be important for the parents and educators to carry over the concepts and strategies that the children learn in the sessions to assist with generalizing their skills. Each lesson will have an accompanying homework assignment to be completed and returned the following week. Please take the time to complete the homework and promote situations throughout the week that help foster the concepts learned in the sessions. The vocabulary and concepts used in this curriculum should provide the support team with additional positive opportunities to reinforce the skills learned by the child. Remember to keep the learning fun and positive! Really try to find those times where your child is being **Superflex** and using his or her strategies to think about others. This will help the child recognize the expected behaviors and make him or her feel good and motivated to continue using the strategies. This can be done with positive reinforcement such as social praise. Enough cannot be said about the power of positive reinforcement!

Below are some examples of how to reinforce these new concepts at home with your child.

- ✿ "I liked that you defeated **Rock Brain** by using your **Superflex Strategy**. That made me feel proud. How do you feel?"
- ✿ "You really worked hard at keeping those hurtful thoughts in your head; nice job, **Superflex!**"
- ✿ "Okay, a **Superflexible** moment is coming up. Let's see if you can defeat **Rock Brain** and shut your video game off. Way to go **Superflex!**"
- ✿ "Hey Sam, you did a great job defeating your **Unthinkable, Rock Brain**, today when you let Jimmy go first."
- ✿ "Tom, nice job defeating the **Body Snatcher** while we were walking together in the store. I felt like you were really thinking about me."
- ✿ It may also be fun to identify when we notice **Unthinkables** taking over the brains of others. If you notice a situation, you can talk about it after the fact. For example, did you notice when **Brain Eater** distracted your dad's brain at dinner?
- ✿ At dinner time, a parent could "plant" an **Unthinkable**, have it show up in their brain, and see if their son or daughter notices. Maybe he or she could even help them with a strategy to defeat their **Unthinkable.**

Superflex®: A Superhero Social Thinking Curriculum
Think Social Publishing, Inc. ©2008 www.socialthinking.com

SuperFlex® Training Academy

Quiet Please-Training In Session!

Hours:
Monday-Friday
8:00 A.M. – 5:00 P.M.

Saturday
8:00 A.M. – 12:00 Noon

Sunday
Out saving Social Town and practicing our Superflex Strategies!

We will return on Monday.

Purpose: The group continues to explore the concepts of **Superflexible thinking*** and Rock Brain thinking by learning about the role of the brain, using a multi- modality approach. They will identify the power of the brain and how the brain assists us, from the body's physical movement to its social tasks, including; learning and recalling factual and social information; understanding how to move our bodies; what to say when around another; and how to see "the big picture" to be an effective problem-solver. The complexity of this lesson will depend on the age of the students. For students ages 4-7, exploration should include where the brain is and a simple discussion on its tasks (thinking, knowing, and remembering information about the world and about others).

Vocabulary:

Superflex
Strategies
Rock Brain
Hidden rules*
Social smarts*
Science smarts*

Goals:

✧ The student will be able to identify two social functions of the brain with _____ accuracy in a structured setting.

✧ The student will be able to identify two social functions that are a strength and a weakness for the student with ___ accuracy.

✧ The student will be able to identify three items in the environment that represent "flexible" and "not-so-flexible" properties with ___ accuracy.

What you need to do before the lesson:

✓ Prior to the session, make a gelatin brain and implant pieces of laminated written examples of brain function.
(See Diagram #1, page 32)
Examples may include:

- 🐾 Helps us move our legs
- 🐾 Helps us move our arms
- 🐾 Helps us breathe
- 🐾 Helps us figure out **hidden rules***
- 🐾 Helps us **think about others***
- 🐾 Helps us make good choices
- 🐾 Helps us know what to do with our eyes when around others
- 🐾 Helps us know what to do with our body when around others
- 🐾 Helps us know what to do with our words when around others
- 🐾 Helps us remember information-memory
- 🐾 Helps us recall details and facts
- 🐾 Remembers facts or details about another's interest

✓ Get capes and **flexible thinking*** brains ready!

Lesson #2 Superflexible Thinking vs. Rock Brain Thinking Dr. Superflex

Materials

Three or four foam brains

Capes

Brain gelatin mold (Amazon.com)

Diagram #1

Plastic hard brain to represent Rock Brain thinking (you can use the plastic Brain Gelatin Mold) or just a hard surface

Tweezers

Latex gloves (make sure your students do not have a latex allergy)

Handout, Lesson #2

Funwork, Lesson #2

🐾 **Caution - DO NOT** bring a rock to the group to represent Rock Brain. Rocks can easily be thrown and can result in injury!

*Refer to pages 15-17 for definition.

29

Superflex®: A Superhero Social Thinking Curriculum
Think Social Publishing, Inc. ©2008 www.socialthinking.com

Teacher Review-Superflex Training Session #2:

1. Place the gelatin brain on the table and make sure you have access to a hard surface (the table would also work) or a hard plastic brain.

2. Explain to the group that today they will be learning about the brain and two ways that we can think with our brains; **Superflexible thinking*** and Rock Brain thinking.

3. Have the students don the latex gloves and then show the children the two examples of brains (soft and hard). Explore how the soft one feels, its properties and why it has these properties and can move. (Because it needs to move and adjust to the world and people around it, this brain can easily shift its thinking to consider other people or what may be happening around them.)

4. Contrast the hard brain or hard surface and examine how sturdy and inflexible this item is. Allow the children to manipulate and poke at the two examples of the brains.

5. Have them make some guesses about what type of thinking happens in the flexible brain versus the brain that is hard and immovable. Point out that Superflex is working hard in the flexible brain and the hard brain is being defeated by Rock Brain. The Rock Brain represents someone's brain who has a hard time shifting and changing his or her thinking. This brain wants to do mainly what it wants to do or think about things only in the moment without looking at the whole picture. This brain does not always think about others or anyone around it.

6. Tell them that in order to be Superflex, one must have a good understanding of the brain, so the group will now learn about the important roles of the brain and identify what their brains do well and what their brains have some trouble with. The children can share their knowledge of the brain with the group, but be careful because some children may just take over your session with their knowledge.

7. Pass out Diagram #1 to the children and review. To simplify the task, explain the Brain jobs have been divided into three categories; how it helps with physical movement; how it helps with **social smarts*** (skills necessary for social success); and how it helps us with **science smarts*** (skills necessary for most academic success).

8. Allow the children, one at a time, to use the tweezers to pull out a strip of paper and read it out loud.

9. While the children share their findings and the group determines what category the skill goes into, the educator can write the information down on an extra handout that can be copied at the end of the session for the families.

10. Encourage the children to provide specific examples after they read their paper strip aloud. For example, if the child selects arm movements, the children can all provide an example of arm movements while the group members copy.

The complexity of this task will obviously differ depending on the age of the children you are working with. For younger children, you can simply create pictures and simplify the language for this activity.

*Refer to pages 15-17 for definition.

30

11. Introduce Handout #2, Rock Brain, and review his powers and how he can be defeated.
12. Time to pass out Superflex Awards!

Funwork, Lesson #2:

Ask that the family help the child explore **flexible*** and Rock Brain thinking further over the week. Also, pass out and review the Rock Brain handout so they are aware of how this character presents itself. Encourage families at this point to limit their comments when they notice Rock Brain is hanging out in their child's brain!

*Refer to pages 15-17 for definition.

Superflex®: A Superhero Social Thinking Curriculum
Think Social Publishing, Inc. ©2008 www.socialthinking.com

Diagram #1

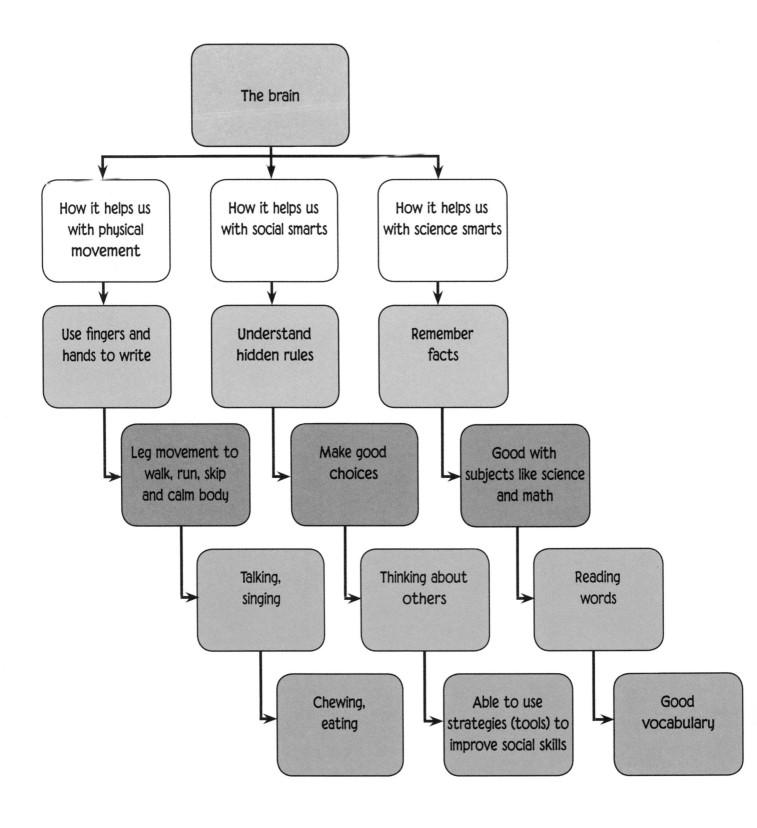

Lesson 2 : Superflexible Thinking vs. Rock Brain Thinking

Superflex®: A Superhero Social Thinking Curriculum
Think Social Publishing, Inc. ©2008 www.socialthinking.com

Rock Brain is on the Loose...

AND HE WANTS TO GET INTO BRAINS
EVERYWHERE TO TAKE OVER YOUR SOCIAL TOWN!!

Be on the lookout for this character!
He may be **hiding** somewhere
in your brain.

He is **very sneaky** and has
defeated *Superflex*® before!!

Do you recognize him?

HE MAY TRY TO:

- Get you stuck on doing only what you want to do.
- He will not let you compromise with others.
- **Rock Brain** will try to make sure that you make only bad choices so a problem only gets worse, or he will get you to try one solution that's not working over and over again.
- He will make you get stuck on rules and get stuck on ways that you want to do things without thinking about others.

If you recognize this character call on your *Superflex* for some *Superflexible strategies* to defeat **Rock Brain**... Here are a few strategies:

Notice that what you are doing is not working and **try another way** to solve the same problem.

Remember that being a part of a group means that you cannot always do it your way or have everything that you want. **Use self-talk:** "Not a problem. I will get to do this later or maybe another time."

Try to think about others' plans and **adjust your thinking** to match their plans.

33

Superflex®: A Superhero Social Thinking Curriculum
Think Social Publishing, Inc. ©2008 www.socialthinking.com

The Hunt for Superflex ®

This week you learned about different types of thinking- **Superflexible** thinking and **Rock Brain** (Not-So-Flexible) Thinking. In our session, we experimented with the difference between items that were soft/flexible **JUST LIKE OUR Superflexible Brains** and items that were **Hard** and did not move, much like those brains invaded by **Rock Brain.** Now take a look around your house and see if you can find some more items that help us think about these concepts.

List or draw three items in your house that are flexible and can change their shapes to represent **Flexible Thinking.**

1.

2.

3.

List or draw three items in your house that are not so flexible and have a hard surface, to represent **Rock Brain Thinking.**

1.

2.

3.

NOW search for someone who is showing signs of **Superflexible Thinking.** What did he or she do?

NOW search for someone who is showing signs of **Rock Brain Thinking.** What did he or she do?

34

Superflex®: A Superhero Social Thinking Curriculum
Think Social Publishing, Inc. ©2008 www.socialthinking.com

Purpose: To continue their exploration into how their brain assists them in doing such things as **thinking about others*** and problem solving. They will do this by learning specifically about one of Superflex's greatest nemeses, Rock Brain, and how this character can impede their ability to think about others! The group will discuss six Superflexible behaviors, some examples of what Superflexible strategies may be used, and how these behaviors may present themselves if Superflex is not able to defeat Rock Brain, resulting in a Rock Brain moment. The emphasis will be on helping them to see how, at a very basic step of **thinking about others*** and taking perspective, one must be grounded in **flexible thinking*** to consider what others are thinking.

Vocabulary:

Superflexible moment
Superflex strategy
Rock Brain moment
Thinking about someone's "plan"
Thinking with your eyes*
Whole Body Listening*
Social wondering*
Hidden rules*
Expected and Unexpected behaviors*
Tiny or Earthquake problem*

Materials:

Social Scenes 1-6 (Appendix D)

Capes

Foam brain(s)

Hard brain

Handout, Lesson #3

Funwork, Lesson #3

Video recording device

Goals:

☆ The students will be able to identify two Superflexible moments that they have demonstrated with others with ___% accuracy.

☆ The students will be able to identify two Rock Brain moments they have demonstrated with others with ___% accuracy.

☆ The students will be able to identify two of six Superflexible behaviors and draw or write a corresponding picture with ___% accuracy.

What you need to do before the lesson:

✓ Cut out pictures from Appendix D and laminate if possible.

✓ Get those capes and flexible brains ready.

Teacher Review-Superflex Training #3:

1. Explain to the children that now that they have a better understanding of the brain and the wonderful things it helps us do, they are going to learn more about this Rock Brain character and what it might look like if Rock Brain is successful in plotting his demise of Superflex. This is a crucial training if we are going to be able to call on Superflex to defeat Rock Brain.

*Refer to pages 15-17 for definition.

2. Tell the students that today they will be learning about six major Superflexible behaviors that our brains can do and what it looks like when Rock Brain takes over and defeats Superflex.

3. Starting with picture #1, introduce the Superflexible behavior while showing Side A (Superflexible moment) and review the Superflexible strategy that was used. The children then can make a guess about what a Rock Brain moment might look like. Show Side B to see if they guessed correctly.

4. The group can videotape and role-play the scenes on each picture, or come up with another version of a Superflexible moment or Rock Brain moment for each picture.

Table 2-Social Scenarios

Social Scene Picture	*Superflexible Behavior*	Superflexible Moment	Superflex Strategy	Rock Brain Moments
1 	*Thinking about others* (what someone else is thinking and feeling) and the expected* behaviors.*	**A.** CHILD KEEPS HIS HURTFUL THOUGHTS IN HIS BRAIN AND SAYS, "OKAY" WHEN HIS MOTHER ASKS HIM TO COME IN FOR DINNER.	✓CHILD THINKS ABOUT HOW HIS WORDS MAY HURT MOM'S FEELINGS. ✓**THINK ABOUT MOM'S PLAN*.**	**B.** CHILD BLURTS OUT THAT HIS MOM IS MEAN AND NEVER LETS HIM PLAY WITH HIS FRIENDS, AND HE CONTINUES TO PLAY.
2 	*Being able to STOP what you are doing and follow what others are asking you to do.*	**A.** CHILD PICKS UP HIS BLOCKS AS SOON AS HE HEARS THE TEACHER SAY, "IT IS TIME TO CLEAN UP."	✓CHILD THINKS ABOUT HOW OTHERS MAY BE LATE TO LUNCH, HOW FRUSTRATED HIS TEACHER MAY FEEL IF HE CONTINUES TO PLAY AND THAT HE MAY GET TO PLAY BLOCKS TOMORROW.	**B.** CHILD CONTINUES TO PLAY EVEN THOUGH HE KNOWS IT IS TIME TO GO TO LUNCH.
3	*During play, shift and adjust thinking to match what others are thinking; helping you stay connected.*	**A.** THE CHILDREN ARE CREATING A ZOO WITH BLOCKS. ONE CHILD SEES THAT ONE BOY IS MAKING THE CAGES FOR THE TIGERS. HE REPLIES, " I CAN MAKE THE CAGE FOR THE LIONS."	✓CHILD **"THINKS WITH HIS EYES*"** TO FIGURE OUT THE PLAN AND THEN ADDS HIS THOUGHTS. ✓CHILD THINKS TO HIMSELF, " I REALLY LIKE MY FACTORIES BUT I NEED TO THINK ABOUT WHAT OTHERS WANT TO PLAY. I CAN BUILD MY FACTORIES LATER."	**B.** THE CHILD IS VERY INTERESTED IN FACTORIES AND INSISTS THAT THE OTHERS BUILD A PART TO HIS FACTORY.

*Refer to pages 15-17 for definition.

36

Social Scene Picture	Superflexible Behavior	Superflexible Moment	Superflex Strategy	Rock Brain Moments
4 	*Shifting and adjusting our thinking to keep others sharing their ideas and having a good time.*	**A.** CHILD LISTENS TO WHAT THE OTHER STUDENTS ARE TALKING ABOUT AND ASKS ANOTHER CHILD A QUESTION RELATED TO THE TOPIC.	✓ CHILD **LISTENS WITH HIS WHOLE BODY*** TO FIGURE OUT THE TOPIC AND THEN ADDS A THOUGHT OR ASKS A QUESTION (**social wondering***).	**B.** CHILD CONTINUES TO BRING UP HIS FAVORITE TOPIC OF CARS EVEN THOUGH THE GROUP IS TRYING TO TALK ABOUT SOMETHING DIFFERENT.
5 	*Being able to stop and look at a problem and the variety of choices that one can use to solve it.*	**A.** CHILD GOES OVER TO THE BOY AND ASKS IF HE CAN TAKE A TURN, AND THEN WAITS PATIENTLY.	✓ CHILD **THINKS ABOUT THE SIZE OF THE PROBLEM*** (tiny or earthquake size) AND IF HE ASKS AND WAITS FOR HIS TURN, HE WILL GET TO RIDE THE BIKE.	**B.** CHILD GOES OVER AND PULLS ON THE BIKE WHILE YELLING THAT HE WANTS TO TAKE A TURN.
6 	*Thinking about what is expected* depending on where you are, what you are doing and who is there.*	**A.** PEOPLE ARE IN A WAITING ROOM READING BOOKS AND MAGAZINES, SO THE CHILD PICKS UP A BOOK AND QUIETLY SITS DOWN.	✓ CHILD **THINKS WITH HIS EYES*** TO FIGURE OUT WHAT OTHERS ARE DOING AND **WHAT IS EXPECTED*** SO THAT HE CAN MATCH THE BEHAVIOR OF THE OTHER PEOPLE.	**B.** CHILD IS IN A WAITING ROOM LOUDLY BOUNCING HIS BALL AND ASKING OTHERS TO JOIN HIM.

5. After they complete this activity, pretend to want to show them some more pictures, but you are unable to find them and realize they have mysteriously disappeared! Then you come across Handout #3 which, in a note from the principal, explains that the Unthinkables have managed to get hold of the pictures. Then work with the students to create more examples of Superflexible and Rock Brain moments.

Funwork, Lesson #3:

Pass out the handout and show the families the Social Scenarios that were explored in the group. Ask that they work with their child to generate more examples to role-play. Encourage the families to videotape the scenes and watch them with their child.

☀ Remind families to have their child bring a bottle of water and a small towel. They will be working out at the Superflex Academy Gym next week!

*Refer to pages 15-17 for definition.

Dear Students,

We need your help, *Superflex*® students! The *Team Of Unthinkables*

are at it again. They have managed to get hold of some of our materials at our school in an attempt to stop us from training more superheroes!! They got hold of some of our secret pictures from this lesson, probably to try and prevent us from teaching these skills to our Superflex students. Since you have just learned about *Superflexible* behaviors, we are asking that our students provide some more picture examples of *Superflexible* moments and *Rock Brain* moments that they have experienced or witnessed. You can write or draw the information. We can then add your scenes when we train our new students next year.

Thank you for your help,

Mr. Flecks

Mr. Flecks
Principal of Superflex Academy

Superflexible Behavior:	Superflexible Strategy:
Superflexible Moment:	Rock Brain Moment:

38

FUNWORK, LESSON #3

With members of your family, pick two *Superflexible* behaviors to role-play. You can make up your own scene or use one that you have already learned about today. Decide who in the group will play what role and what the *Superflexible* strategy will be. Also, after you role-play the scene, write down how others felt in the scene when they were around someone who was having a *Rock Brain* moment versus a *Superflexible* moment.

Superflexible Behavior	*Superflexible* Moment	*Superflex®* Strategy	How did others around him/her feel?	*Rock Brain* Moment	How did others around him/her feel?
1					
2					

Superflexible Behaviors

@ Thinking about others (someone else's point of view) and expected behaviors.

@ Being able to STOP what you want to do and adjust to what is required of you.

@ During play, changing your thinking to match what others are thinking to stay connected and to keep others feeling good.

@ Shifting and adjusting your thinking to keep others sharing their ideas and having a good time.

@ Being able to stop and look at a problem and the variety of choices that one can use to solve the problem.

@ Thinking about the hidden rules and expectations in different environments.

39

Superflex®: A Superhero Social Thinking Curriculum
Think Social Publishing, Inc. ©2008 www.socialthinking.com

Purpose: To reinforce the idea that the children have the ability to make their brains be Superflexible. Many students will argue that they are not in control of their thinking or their behavior; however, once you complete several tasks requiring the students to shift their thinking and adjust to the thinking of others, this point is moot!

Vocabulary:

Superflexible thinking*
Superflexible strategy
Rock Brain thinking

Goals:

☆ The student will demonstrate **flexible thinking*** by changing his thinking when given a "mixed up" direction with ___% accuracy.

☆ The student will be able to identify **flexible thinking*** and not-so-flexible thinking in other students with ___% accuracy.

What you need to do before the lesson:

✓ Hang the Superflex Academy Gym sign on treatment room door.

✓ Place 3-5 pieces of obstacle course equipment throughout the treatment room.

✓ Get capes and **flexible thinking*** brains ready!

Teacher Review-Superflex Training #4:

1. Begin the session by explaining that one of Superflex's powers is **flexible thinking***. This part of the brain is very strong. To be the ultimate Superflex, we all must strengthen and practice this type of thinking because it will help us in defeating our team of Unthinkables! A Superflex brain will have no problem shifting and adjusting its thinking to think about someone else, or stopping its body and doing something completely different with no problem.

2. Tell the children that you will be doing several Superflex exercises at the Superflex Academy Gym to see if their brains have the control and strength needed to move on to the next Superflex lessons. The tasks will test their brain power to see if they can demonstrate **flexible thinking***, and they will be given an overall grade at the end of the session.

3. Pass out Handout Lesson #4 and review.

4. Place the obstacle course items throughout the room and tell the kids that they will take turns going through this training.

5. Have the children put on their Superflex capes and take their picture separately. These pictures will be used in a later lesson.

Materials:

Superflex Academy Gym sign (page 44)

Obstacle course materials (small trampoline, spinner, tunnel, large treatment ball, etc.)

Capes

Flexible brain

Rock brain

Digital camera

Photo paper

Bottles of water and towels for each student

Handout, Lesson #4

Funwork, Lesson #4

*Refer to pages 15-17 for definition.

40

6. When the first person is ready, tell the students that they will be doing an obstacle course BUT they will have to follow "mixed up" directions to ensure that their Superflexible brains are really getting a workout.

> *"Johnny please go and jump 15 times on the trampoline. Shortly after he begins this task, ask him to stop and begin another task on another item. "Oh, forget it Johnny, go and bounce the ball 20 times." Repeat this pattern until the child has been to all the activities, making sure that he does NOT complete one task. Ask the child how he did at being a Superflexible thinker and compliment his job at shifting his thinking and behavior!*

7. Hold up the flexible brain and the ROCK BRAIN and ask the group whether this child was using his **Superflexible thinking*** or his Rock Brain thinking to get through the task? Then, give the child the flexible-thinking brain to hold onto until the next child completes the activity.

8. Have the child write his results on his handout. If the activity is being videotaped, then the handouts can be completed when all the activities are done.

9. Continue the activity until all the children have had an opportunity to do the obstacle course and the others have commented on their performance.

10. Do two or three more activities that require the students to demonstrate their **flexible thinking***, and record their performance on the handout. Some additional activities are listed:
    a. Building a tower with only one designer so everyone has to be flexible with one child's plan.
    b. Play a simple board game and highlight the Superflexible moments such as deciding on what the group will play, who will go first, being in last or second to last place, etc.
    c. Walk around with your group and change your mind on where you are going and what you are doing, and see how they adjust.
    d. Bring in ingredients for a simple snack and have them create snacks for others while providing mixed-up directions.

11. Time to pass out the weekly Superflex Awards!

Funwork Lesson #4:

The Superflex Family: Explain that Superflexible powers must run in the family, and they will be in charge of finding this out. The child will work with his family and do various activities that will involve **Superflexible thinking***. The child will record his findings on his Superhero Report Card and return to the Superflex instructor the following week.

If a child has difficulty completing this activity because he is so rigid, give him a break, and then when he returns, give him a direction that is not desirable. "Johnny, do 100 pushups," then quickly switch direction, "100 situps." Then complete the activity once you have success and he has demonstrated some level of flexible thinking.

*Refer to pages 15-17 for definition.

41

Do YOU have what it takes?

Today we will be doing some tests at the *Superflex® Academy Gym* to see if you are a good candidate for our *Superflex* training. In order to become the ultimate superhero, *Superflex*, one must have some ability to control his behavior. After each activity, you and your teacher will put a grade on your Brain Test form. You will receive a **Pass (P)** or **Needs More Work (NMW)** for your final grade. If you receive a P, then you may continue on with the rest of the training sessions at the academy. If you receive a NMW, you may be asked to do more brain exercises to strengthen your thinking.

Brain Exercises

Name		
Activities:	Did the student demonstrate flexible thinking on this task?	**Grade:** PASS (P)= *Able to do activity without help.* NEEDS MORE WORK (NMW)=*could not do it.*
Activity #1		
Activity #2		
Activity #3		
Total Grade		

Please send a copy of grade to the school principal, Mr. Flecks. This report will be added to your student file. Keep up the great work, *Superflex* students!

Thank you,

Mr. Flecks

Mr. Flecks, Principal

42

Superflex® Family Report Card

Grade your family on their *Superflexible* Thinking skills. After each activity, give a **P=Pass** (did it) or a **NMW=Needs More Work** (could not do it) grade and return to your teacher at the *Superflex Academy* next week.

Family Member	Activity #1 Followed "mixed-up" directions at the park on the equipment. (circle one below)	Activity #2 Followed "mixed-up" directions in the kitchen when making a meal or snack. (circle one below)	Activity #3 Followed "mixed-up" directions in an activity of your choice. (circle one below)	Overall Grade: Pass (P) or Needs More Work (NMW).
Superflex (you)	YES NO	YES NO	YES NO	
	YES NO	YES NO	YES NO	
	YES NO	YES NO	YES NO	

Does *Superflexible* thinking run in your family? (circle one) **Yes**   **NO**

CAUTION!!! Be Aware that parents do not always have to use their Superflexible thinking. Because they are the parents, they are responsible for their children's safety and health and have to make major decisions about the family, which may mean that they have to stick to a decision they feel is best for the family. Can you think of an example when they may not be able to use their flexible thinking?

43

Superflex®: A Superhero Social Thinking Curriculum
Think Social Publishing, Inc. ©2008 www.socialthinking.com

Superflex® Academy
Gym

Hours:

MONDAY-FRIDAY 7:00 A.M.-7:00 P.M.
SATURDAY-SUNDAY 8:00 A.M.-5:00 P.M.

MUST BE A STUDENT OR TEACHER
AT THE SUPERFLEX ACADEMY TO ENTER!!!

Rules:

✋ PLEASE PUT THE EQUIPMENT BACK AFTER YOU USE IT.

✋ PLEASE BE CAREFUL WITH YOUR CAPE. WE CANNOT REPLACE IT IF IT GETS TORN.

✋ PLEASE TAKE TURNS ON THE EQUIPMENT IF SOMEONE IS WAITING.

✋ PLEASE BRING YOUR OWN TOWEL AND WATER.

44

Superflex®: A Superhero Social Thinking Curriculum
Think Social Publishing, Inc. ©2008 www.socialthinking.com

Purpose: Now that your students are more familiar with the differences between **Superflexible thinking*** and Rock Brain thinking, continue to explore and identify these situations through role playing. Now your students get to play the part of Superflex! The children will truly enjoy this lesson because they are getting the chance to be their own Superflex superhero, and get to practice defeating their first Unthinkable, Rock Brain.

Vocabulary:

Tiny or big problem
Superflex
Superflexible strategy
Rock Brain

Goals:

⭐ While role-playing, the student will generate and demonstrate knowledge of one strategy to defeat Rock Brain with ___% accuracy.

⭐ While role-playing, the student will be able to provide a Superflexible strategy to defeat Rock Brain.

⭐ During the session, the student will demonstrate **Superflexible thinking***, with use of one strategy, during structured tasks with ___% accuracy.

Materials:

Dizzy disc, trampoline or nylon tunnel

Capes

Rock Brain

Superflex Brain

Video recording device

Cell phone or office phone

Handout, Lesson #5

Funwork, Lesson #5

Teacher Review-Superflex Training Session #5:

1. Begin to get the children started on their lesson for the day, but while doing this pretend the Principal of SF Academy is calling on the phone to say that the Superflex Brain Sensor in his office is alerting him that there is a Superflex emergency!

2. Nervously verbalize one of the Rock Brain moments from last week's session (Table #2). For example, "Oh my gosh, Mr. Flecks, the Superflex brain is vibrating? And it is saying that there is a child who is at school playing with his blocks, and his teacher has asked the class to get ready for lunch? Don't worry, sir! I have just the Superflex to handle this job! We will take care of it!"

3. Select one of the group members to be Superflex and the other members to be the actors in the scene.

4. Hand the Superflexible brain to the student portraying Superflex and the Rock Brain to the not-so-flexible character in the scene. Before you begin the scene, have Superflex generate a strategy that he will use to defeat Rock Brain.

5. Make sure that the characters know their roles and then ask the child selected to play Superflex to don his cape and jump 3 times on the trampoline to transform into Superflex.

6. Superflex then pretends to fly around Social Town looking for the child whose brain is being taken over by Rock Brain. Once Superflex finds the child holding the Rock Brain, he can whisper the strategy in their

Videotape the scenes so the children can watch themselves in action!

*Refer to pages 15-17 for definition.

45

Superflex®: A Superhero Social Thinking Curriculum
Think Social Publishing, Inc. ©2008 www.socialthinking.com

Videotape the scenes so the children can watch themselves in action!

ear, switch the Rock Brain for the Superflex Brain, and fly away. Once this happens the scene continues, only this time the boy is making good choices and using his strategy to be Superflexible.

7. Give each of the children an opportunity to be Superflex with a new Rock Brain moment. Make sure that each new Superflex Mission is called in by the principal.

8. Using Handout #5, watch the videotape and discuss how others in the scene were feeling and thinking when there was a Rock Brain moment versus a Superflex moment, how the child did at using the Superflex strategy, and how others felt once Rock Brain was defeated.

9. Hand out Superflex awards for their hard work today at the academy.

Funwork Lesson #5:

Have the children identify a time when they noticed a Rock Brain moment coming on but managed to defeat him, thanks to their own Superflex and Superflexible strategy.

Superflex®: A Superhero Social Thinking Curriculum
Think Social Publishing, Inc. ©2008 www.socialthinking.com

How Did Superflex® Do?

Practice, Practice, Practice! You will have other opportunities to become *Superflex*, but let's see how you did on your first mission. Watch the video and rate your performance. Please return these sheets to Mr. Flecks in the office. He and the Mayor of Social Town want to know how you helped out the town.

Dear Mr. Flecks and Mayor of Social Town,

Today, I was successful at helping one of your citizens defeat an **Unthinkable** *UFF* to keep Social Town alive!!

I helped defeat the Unthinkable: _____

The strategy was: _____

Superflex Skills:

You Did It!

I was able to keep the cape on the whole time.

❏ **YES**   ❏ **NO**

I transformed into *Superflex* without any problems (i.e., tripping, falling).

❏ **YES**   ❏ **NO**

I had good flying skills (placed hands out in front, did not get cape caught in anything).

❏ **YES**   ❏ **NO**

I was able to make a good landing (did not fall, bump into anyone, etc.).

❏ **YES**   ❏ **NO**

I used a friendly voice when talking to the citizen.

❏ **YES**   ❏ **NO**

I was able to come up with a *Superflexible Strategy* to assist the citizens of Social Town.

❏ **YES**   ❏ **NO**

I think I did a pretty good job for my first *Superflex* mission. I look forward to many more!!

_____
Superflex student signature

47

Superflex®: A Superhero Social Thinking Curriculum
Think Social Publishing, Inc. ©2008 www.socialthinking.com

Draw a picture or write about a time this week that you called on your *Superflex®* to defeat *Rock Brain!*

Draw a picture of *Rock Brain* and what you think he was thinking while trying to defeat your *Superflex*.

How many times were you *Superflex* this week? Put a star in the box below each time.

Lesson 5 : Your First Superflex® Mission...

Superflex®: A Superhero Social Thinking Curriculum
Think Social Publishing, Inc. ©2008 www.socialthinking.com

Purpose: To continue to explore social challenges that can hinder one's ability to demonstrate good social skills. Children will review and identify the cast of Unthinkable characters who tend to sidetrack people's brains so that they do not take perspective and think about the social world around them. The students will also learn about what specific behaviors (Unthinkables®) invade their own brains.

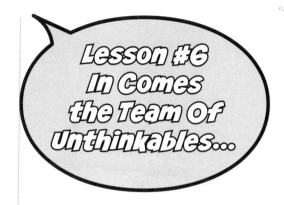

Vocabulary:

Superflex
Superflexible strategies
Team of Unthinkables (See Appendix B)
Expected/Unexpected behaviors *
Smart guess*

Goals:

✨ The students will identify at least three Unthinkable characters (behaviors) that invade their brains and give a specific example for each with ___% success.

✨ The students will be able to identify the Unthinkable Team Leader that invades their brains the most and give an example with ___% accuracy.

✨ The students will be able to identify one Superflexible strategy to defeat each Unthinkable that they have identified, with ___% accuracy.

Materials:
....
Bubbles

Appendix B – Definitions-Superflex and Team of Unthinkables cards

Handout, Lesson #6

Funwork, Lesson #6

Dizzy disc (spinner) or trampoline

Superflex capes

Butcher paper to make a Most-Wanted Unthinkables poster

Piece of butcher paper for group drawing

Velcro

What you need to do before the lesson:

✓ Prior to the session, make a Most Wanted Unthinkables poster using butcher paper and cards from Handout #6. Make 3 columns/14 rows on the butcher paper. The columns should be titled "Unthinkables," "Powers," and "Superflex Strategies." Stick the Unthinkable cards and strategies onto their appropriate place on the poster.

✓ Post the Most Wanted Unthinkable poster on a wall in the room, and place the Unthinkable "Power" cards face down in a location across the room.

Teacher Review-Superflex Training Session #6:

1. Explain to the students that they are now going to be learning more about the team of Unthinkables that like to challenge our brains in social situations and try to prevent us from **thinking about others*** by doing **unexpected*** behaviors or making **not-so-good*** choices.

*Refer to pages 15-17 for definition.

49

Continue to reinforce the great Superflexible thinking you see taking place with your group members.

Is there any furniture or items I need to move to ensure safety?

By this time, inevitably a group member will mention an unexpected behavior that has not been identified with an Unthinkable. Feel free to improvise, at any time, and create a new member of the Team. Encourage the group to work together to give the member a name, its power and what strategies will defeat this new Unthinkable. They may even want to draw the character.

2. Have the children work together to do a group drawing on paper of what Social Town might look like if the Unthinkables took over and defeated Superflex.

   ◉ During this mini lesson, the children take turns drawing different community locations (library, playground, etc.) on butcher paper and what the citizens might be saying if an Unthinkable is in their brain. This activity should provide an opportunity to emphasize what citizens in our own town do to defeat the Unthinkables. How do we feel when we go to the playground or library if people are defeating their Unthinkables?

3. Hang the completed group drawing across the room from the Most Wanted Unthinkables Poster. The students will use this drawing to represent Social Town during the following activity.

4. Introduce the Unthinkable Characters listed on the poster. Encourage them to make guesses about what they think their "powers" might be. Explain that their next mission is to fly safely to Social Town to uncover the Team of Unthinkable "power" cards, and then return to the Academy so we can complete the list. This sounds easy; however, they will need to work together as a group and help each Superflex maneuver through a bubble meteor shower. If the student is touched by a meteor, he will have to start all over again. The other students can cheer and direct Superflex on his mission.

5. Select one student to put on his cape and spin him three times on the dizzy disc or trampoline to transform into Superflex. Now the child must get to the other side of the room while you are blowing bubbles across his path.

6. Once the child successfully brings back an Unthinkable "power" card, have him read the information and make a guess about which Unthinkable would have this power. Take time to introduce the Superflexible Strategies that can then defeat this power.

7. Give another student a turn to go on his mission to bring back an Unthinkable "power" card. Continue until all "power" cards are on the poster.

8. Once the list is completed, the group can complete Handout #6, My Team Of Unthinkables.

9. Have the students identify their Team of Unthinkables from the list. They can draw their own versions of these characters, glue on copies of the Unthinkable cards or simply write in the name. I encourage the educators to also complete their own Team of Unthinkables handout with the students.

   ◉ Explain to the students that there is usually one Unthinkable that hangs out in our brain more than the others, and this character is usually the TEAM LEADER.

10. As a group, go through and review everyone's TEAM LEADER and then ask the students to identify and write down a strategy from the list (you may also generate additional strategies that are not listed).

50

11. Make a copy of each child's completed Team Of Unthinkable handout so you can display and use them as visual cues in future sessions.

Funwork, Lesson #6:

Hand out copies of Appendix B, Definitions-Superflex and Team of Unthinkables cards. The handout used in Lesson #6 will also be used as a funwork assignment. Ask that it be posted on the refrigerator where it can provide a constant reminder about Superflex's challenges and strategies. Have the child and parents monitor when Superflex was able to defeat one of the Unthinkables during the week. Remind parents that the homework is not to identify when an Unthinkable is present but to catch the child demonstrating **Superflexible thinking*** to defeat an Unthinkable. This will foster a more positive experience for the child while still increasing his awareness of the Unthinkables. The child's teacher or paraprofessional can also provide input and insight into the child's self-awareness and use of strategies.

On this page are some examples on how to provide a positive prompt when those Unthinkable moments come up. . .

WOW! I loved how you used your strategy and compromised with me.

Nice job, Superflex! I liked how you told Tommy that you tried your best and congratulated him. I bet that made him feel really good.

"I think **Mean Jean / Gene** is hanging out right now; how could you say that differently to defeat her or him?? How about keeping those bossy words in your brain? That might be something to try next time."

This looks like a flexible-thinking moment. How can you defeat **Rock Brain**? *Nice job, Superflex!*

"Hey, you could've been bossy with your friend right there and you weren't! *Great job Superflex!* Way to keep that thought in your brain."

I think this may be a job for **Superflex**... What is your strategy when **Glassman** hangs out? *Nice job!* Let's take some deep breaths. *You did it!*

*Refer to pages 15-17 for definition.

51

Table 3

Superflex® and Unthinkable® Definitions and Strategies

Superhero	Superflex's strengths
Superflex	Our hero! Totally flexible, trying to figure out people's wants and needs to keep other people calm while also getting his turn to play and to speak as well.
	Superflex is a great problem-solver and can think of many different solutions to one problem. (Note: in our storybook and curriculum, the Superflex you read about is Aiden's Superflex. Your Superflex looks like you, mine looks like me, etc. Find a fun **Superflex is Me** handout at the end of the book to draw your own Superflex!)

Team of Unthinkables	The "powers" they have over our brains	Superflex Strategies to solve the problem and defeat the Unthinkable
Rock Brain	He will get the person to do only what he wants to do and will not let him negotiate with other people. The person is not a good problem-solver and tries one solution that's not working over and over again. This person may be very rule bound and rigid in his thinking, only seeing one way to a situation.	Notice that what you are doing is not working and try another way to solve the same problem. Take a deep breath and remember that being part of a group means that you cannot always do it your way or make the decisions you want. Self talk: "Not a problem, I will get to do this later or another time…" Ask yourself, "What is their plan?" And then try to match their plan.
Brain Eater	He makes it hard for the person to focus on what he is doing or focus on others during interactions (roll his brain away). The person may get easily distracted with his own thoughts or things around him.	Turn your body and eyes away from what is distracting you and think about the person talking. Use a fidget so that it keeps your body busy but your brain focused on the group. Try to notice when your brain is thinking about something else and get it to refocus on the group.

52

Superflex®: A Superhero Social Thinking Curriculum
Think Social Publishing, Inc. ©2008 www.socialthinking.com

Team of Unthinkables	The "powers" they have over our brains	*Superflex Strategies* to solve the problem and defeat the Unthinkable
Body Snatcher 	He gets the person to wander away from others (roll his body away) and not stay with the group or person he is with. May also get the person to turn his body away from the group, not realizing the message he is sending to others.	Use your eyes to think about where your group is or who is talking to you, and find the group! Self-talk: "Where should my body be?" Point your shoulders to the group.
D.O.F. The Destroyer of Fun 	This character often pops up during games or activities involving competition. The person becomes overly competitive and insists on going first, playing only what he wants to play, and does not think about compromising or about how he makes others feel.	Self-talk: "If I am a **"Just Me*"** player, then my friends will not have a good time." Self-Talk: "Tiny problem. I will still get a turn or may win another time."
Un-Wonderer 	He stops the person from showing interest (social wondering) in others or thinking about what others may want to do. The person may not ask a lot of questions about others or add his ideas to what they are playing.	Look at the person who is talking to let him know that you are thinking about him and what he is saying. Listen to the topic and then ask a "social wonder" question of your friend. Create a **people-file*** in your brain to call on later to ask questions. Remember the Wh-question words and use them to think of questions for your friends.
Space Invader 	This character makes the person's body move into other people's personal space when others are not expecting it or do not want this. He does not realize how uncomfortable this makes others feel.	Use one-arm rule to determine if you are standing too close to someone. Think about what your body looks like in the group. Are you making others have good thoughts or weird thoughts? If you are making others have weird thoughts, adjust your body.

*Refer to pages 15-17 for definition.

53

Team of Unthinkables	The "powers" they have over our brains	*Superflex Strategies* to solve the problem and defeat the Unthinkable
Glassman 	Lets a person be flexible to some extent, but then all of a sudden he just breaks. He doesn't melt down slowly; he quickly starts getting very upset often over "tiny" problems. Glassman usually thinks things aren't "fair."	Identify the size of the problem (1-10) and what would be an expected reaction to match the size of the problem. ___ Self-Talk: "I am starting to get mad. I need to move away and take a break or tighten all of the muscles in my body and then relax them.
Grump Grumpaning 	Makes the person think the worst or feel like people are always unkind. He ends up believing it even when people are trying to be nice. He may also see everything as negative or bad and does not see how his emotion spreads and makes everyone feel unhappy.	Think about how the person treats you. Is he friendly or mean to you? If this person is friendly to me then he is not being mean to me. ___ Self talk: "I am being negative. What could be a positive way to think about it?"
Topic Twistermeister 	This character gets the person to twist the topic around to what he wants to talk about and goes off on tangents when talking to others. This person may then go on and on about topics he wants to talk about, not realizing that others may be bored or disinterested in what he is talking about.	Check-in with those around you. Does it look like they are interested in what you are saying? If not, ask a question about what they might want to talk about. ___ Turn off your "Me" button and try to think only about the other person by asking him questions.
WasFunnyOnce 	This person will attempt to use a lot of humor to be funny. However, he does not realize that humor wears out pretty quickly or at times is not "funny" at all. He has trouble recognizing appropriate times for humor and may try to be funny during a discussion in a classroom or when the moment is serious and not funny or silly. Some people may get so silly, that the other children become silly also making the group fall apart. This is called getting caught up in the "silly tornado."	Self-talk: "Is now a silly moment or a serious moment?" If a serious moment, then this is not a good time to crack a joke or say something that I think is funny. ___ Use the one-time-rule: only say the word or joke once and then move on so that the joke does not get boring for others.

54

Superflex®: A Superhero Social Thinking Curriculum
Think Social Publishing, Inc. ©2008 www.socialthinking.com

Team of Unthinkables	The "powers" they have over our brains	*Superflex Strategies* to solve the problem and defeat the Unthinkable
Energy Hare-y 	This character gives the person so much energy so that he is constantly fidgeting or moving around, and he doesn't think about what the people around him needs or how others are feeling around them. Sometimes, Energy Hare-y and WasFunnyOnce work together, which can quickly make the group fall apart.	When others are talking, use Whole Body Listening (keep your whole body quiet). Check in with your eyes and see how the rest of the group is acting. Try to match how calm the other kids are with their bodies. Take a few deep breaths to calm your body.
One-Sided Sid	This character gets the person to talk about his own set of topics or his own plan. Even when someone else brings up his interests, he just talks about his own interests. He may interrupt to talk about what is on his mind, not seeing that someone may have another plan.	Open your people-file and think about what you know about the person. Ask questions to find out more about him and his experiences or interests. Think with your eyes to figure out what the person's plan is. If he looks busy, save your question for another time. Look for clues that others are not interested: looking away, bored look, trying to change the topic.
Worry Wall	He makes the person worry or feel nervous so much about the people around him or the social situations that he or she "hits a wall" and stops being able to talk at all to the people nearby.	Close your eyes, take a deep breath, and let it out slowly. Continue to do this until your body feels relaxed. Find a thought that can change how you are feeling. "Johnny is nice; he will help me with this."
Mean Jean/Gene 	This person becomes just plain mean to other people. He or she insults or criticizes others. He or she may take things away from them, be very bossy, or hog all the attention when others are trying to talk.	Think about what you are going to say before you say it. Self-talk: "Will this hurt my friend's feelings?" Keep bragging, bossy, or hurtful thoughts in our brains.

55

Superflex®: A Superhero Social Thinking Curriculum
Think Social Publishing, Inc. ©2008 www.socialthinking.com

Name: _____

My UNTHINKABLE® TEAM...

My Unthinkable team leader is:	My Superflex® strategy is:
	Defeated him when...

Unthinkable #2:	Unthinkable #3:	Unthinkable #4:
My Superflex strategy:	My Superflex strategy:	My Superflex strategy:
Defeated him when...	Defeated him when...	Defeated him when..

Lesson 6: In Comes the Team of Unthinkables...

Superflex®: A Superhero Social Thinking Curriculum
Think Social Publishing, Inc. ©2008 www.socialthinking.com

Purpose: To highlight and spend specific time learning more about an Unthinkable that has a tendency to frequent the treatment session, D.O.F. The Destroyer of Fun! It was decided to give this character direct attention due to the fact that many sessions involve some form of game playing or competitive activity that often prove very challenging for many of our students.

Lesson #7 Honorable Mention... D.O.F. The Destroyer of Fun

Vocabulary:

Superflex
D.O.F. The Destroyer of Fun
Superflex strategies
Thinking of Others player
Just Me player
Big problem vs. a tiny problem*

Goals:

☆ The student will be able to list example of situations when D.O.F. may "hang out" with ___% accuracy.

☆ Through role-playing, the student will be able to identify three D.O.F. behaviors in others with ___% accuracy.

☆ Through use of video or in less-structured activities, the student will be able to identify two D.O.F. The Destroyer of Fun "powers" that take over their brains with ___% accuracy.

What you need to do before the lesson:

✓ Get capes and flexible-thinking brains ready!

Materials:

Handout, Lesson #7

Funwork, Lesson #7

Video of a different group playing a game or competitive activity or story (See Appendix A)

Video recording device and T.V.

Teacher Review-Superflex® Training Session #7:

1. As the children enter and sit down at the table, tell the kids in a concerned voice that you just got a message from Superflex headquarters. Start to tell them about the bulletin you received from the principal, and then playfully pause to check outside the room to make sure that no one is eavesdropping. (The kids love this and will most likely want to join in the fun and look outside, too.) Proceed to tell them that you received a bulletin and that the group will be learning more about this Unthinkable in the session today.

2. Review the bulletin with the group, highlighting what powers this character possesses. Spend time reviewing the Superflex Strategies on the handout and ways they can show others they are **thinking about others*** while playing a game.

   ⊚ Specific attention may need to be given to such concepts as negotiating and compromising, being a "Thinking of Others*" player, taking the sting out of losing, and letting everyone take a turn being the loser to explore how big a deal it really is. A "Thinking of Others*" person demonstrates **expected*** behaviors to show others that he is **thinking about the other person***. For more information, see *Think Social!* curriculum.

*Refer to pages 15-17 for definition.

57

Caution: Before showing the video, I stress that the children can only comment on their own behavior unless I am posing a question to the group. This will help eliminate any mean or hurtful comments.

3. Ask the children to give examples of situations when D.O.F. invaded their own or someone else's brain. Role-play these examples and encourage the children to identify when they notice D.O.F. is taking over someone's brain.

4. Explain to the children that they will be doing some training to practice identifying this Unthinkable. Have them watch a video of recent group activities or read a story that is filled with D.O.F. moments.

5. Using Handout, Lesson #7, discuss these D.O.F. moments to explore what happened in the scene and have the children circle the behaviors on the sheet. Discussion could also include;
   a. What was the character thinking?
   b. How were others feeling?
   c. Were their other Unthinkables around?

Funwork Lesson #7:

Have the children practice defeating D.O.F. at home. Encourage the families to have a game night during the week. The parents can model Superflexible strategies and also demonstrate times when their brains get taken over by D.O.F. The children can teach their parents about this character and how to defeat him.

58

Special Bulletin

D.O.F. The Destroyer of Fun
has escaped and is finding his way into Social Thinking groups everywhere!

BEWARE: He is invisible and likes to hang out where there are games, sports, or anything that involves competition.

Let's figure out what his powers are so we know when he shows up and what *Superflex® Strategies* to use to defeat him!

D.O.F. Likes to prevent us or others from having a fun time while playing games. This may include:

- *Not letting us compromise with others*
- *Insisting that we go first or have a specific color during a game*
- *Not being flexible to try new games; only sticking to the games that you know*
- *Changing the rules midway through the game or adding new rules that make the game more complicated*
- *Makes you think problems are huge and gets you to have big reactions*
- *Using mean or unfriendly words or mean tone*
- *Cheating/Peeking at another's card*
- *Bragging*

Can you think of others?

But wait...Superflex Strategies can help by:

- *If you do not get to have something your way during the game, ask yourself, "how big a problem is it?" If a tiny problem, then what is a tiny response: let it go, compromise or negotiate, or pick your next favorite color*
- *Helping to change our brains and the way we think about things so that way we can come up with fair ways to compromise: rock, paper, scissors; roll dice, or everyone just picks a number not already chosen*
- *Switching our brain to see that choosing a new game can be fun as long as the kids around are all having fun*
- *Being flexible and telling ourselves that we tried our best and had fun playing with our friends*
- *Using our words to communicate how we are feeling if we are mad about something*
- *Complimenting others about the great game they had*

Can you think of others?

59

Superflex®: A Superhero Social Thinking Curriculum
Think Social Publishing, Inc. ©2008 www.socialthinking.com

Is D.O.F. The Destroyer of Fun hanging out at your house?

Let's see. Choose a night to have a family game night. This may include a board or card game or playing a sport outside as a family. Tell the family about the **Unthinkable, D.O.F. The Destroyer of Fun**, to make sure that your family members know about this character. Then, while playing the game, keep an eye out for any **D.O.F.** moments! You will want to watch others and see how they are feeling. You can usually tell when **D.O.F.** is hanging out in someone's brain by how others around him are feeling. When **D.O.F.** is around, others playing the game or sport are not having fun!

What might be some clues that others are not having fun or enjoying the game or sport?

1.

2.

3.

Write the "expected" behaviors (**Superflexible** thinking) you observed during the game(s) in the lighter spots on the soccer ball.
Write the "unexpected" behaviors (**D.O.F. The Destroyer of Fun** moments) you observed during the game(s) in the darker spots on the soccer ball.

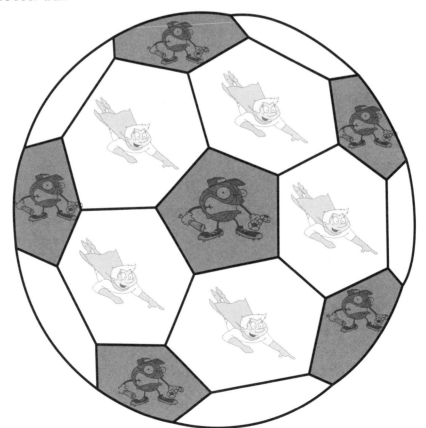

60

Superflex®: A Superhero Social Thinking Curriculum
Think Social Publishing, Inc. ©2008 www.socialthinking.com

Purpose: To increase the student understanding of expectations for being a part of a group; particularly, how to actively listen and listen with one's whole body when in a group. Many of our students have difficulty attending and keeping their brains **thinking about others*** around them. They often become distracted with their own thoughts or, in other instances, items within their environment. Therefore, it may be beneficial to specifically address this Unthinkable and discuss how to defeat him to help limit his presence in the treatment room.

Vocabulary:

Superflex
Superflex strategies
Brain Eater
Whole Body Listening*
Keeping brain and/or body in the group*
Brain rolling out of the group and/or body out of the group*
Distracter: Anything that gets the brain to change and focus on
    something else

Goals:

☆ The students will be able to describe how others may feel if the Brain Eater gets into their brains and identify two strategies to defeat this Unthinkable with ____% accuracy.

☆ The student will be able to demonstrate **Whole Body Listening*** and demonstrate this skill during structured tasks with ____% accuracy.

☆ The student will be able to identify two strategies to defeat Brain Eater and demonstrate during various tasks with ____% accuracy.

What you need to do before the lesson:

✓ On separate Post it® notes, write each distracter (i.e., video game, book, etc.) you have chosen to use in the session. On the back of the Post it® note, write a related scene to role-play later in the session.

✓ Make sure the examples of distracter items are set up to use.

✓ Get capes and flexible-thinking brains ready!

Teacher Review-Superflex® Training Session #8:

1. Greet the students and express a sense of urgency to get them into the room. Once they are in, sigh and tell them "It's happened again." When they ask, "What?" show them the Special Bulletin on the Brain Eater. "Another Unthinkable is on the loose! Principal Flecks has added a special training for the students at the Academy to make sure that you know how to defeat this Unthinkable."

Materials:
....

Handout, Lesson #8

Funwork, Lesson #8

Highly motivating distracters:

Movie, Game Boy, Legos, computer games, kids' magazines or video game magazines, etc.

Butcher paper

Post it® notes

*Refer to pages 15-17 for definition.

61

2. Explain to the children that first they are to make a replica of the Brain Eater out of butcher paper. Brain Eater can be drawn or butcher paper could be crumpled and manipulated into the shape of an octopus. After the octopus is made, spend time exploring what items or topics their Brain Eater uses to distract them. Have the children write down three items on separate Post it® notes and place them on the tentacles of the character.

3. Add your additional Post it® notes to the octopus and tell the students that they are going to go through training to help them work on recognizing when this Unthinkable gets into their brain.

4. Review the list of strategies to defeat the Brain Eater and select one child to do the training first.

5. Have the child select a Post it® note off the Brain Eater and generate a strategy he would like to use to defeat the Brain Eater. Let the child decide whether he would like to act out the Superflexible moment or Brain Eater moment first. When the children can successfully use a strategy to defeat the Unthinkable, they can permanently remove the appropriate Post it® note from the Brain Eater. The goal of this training is to remove as many distracters off the Brain Eater as possible.

Funwork, Lesson #8:

Ask parents to assist their child as they go on a hunt through their house to locate items or to brainstorm topics that tend to distract their children. Ask them to return the handout to share next week with the group.

Examples of role-playing scenarios:

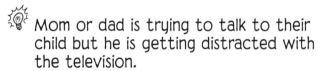 Mom or dad is trying to talk to their child but he is getting distracted with the television.

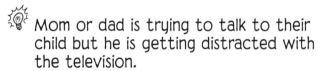 Two kids are playing a board game, but one boy really wants to play with the Legos© that he sees on the shelf.

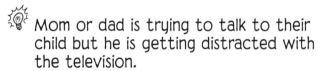 The child is sitting in a group and there is a rubber chicken in front of him that he REALLY wants to play with.

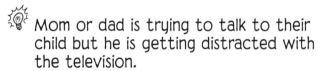 Two children are talking about school and one boy really wants to talk about his video game magazine.

Special Bulletin

He may be disguised as other sea life, like a shark or squid!

Have you seen this character—
Brain Eater?
Be on the lookout, because he is finding his way into brains everywhere!

BEWARE: He may be armed with several distracters! He will do what he has to in order to distract your brain so that you are not thinking about others around you. Other tricks that Brain Eater has been known to try are:

- *Getting your brain to think about your favorite interest*
- *Trying to show videos or pictures in your brain that may be fun to think about, even though others may be trying to talk to you and your group*
- *Getting your brain to talk about what you are thinking about, even though it may not be on topic*
- *Getting your brain to focus on items in front of you and even get you to grab the objects in front of you (i.e., a pencil or book, etc.)*

CAN YOU THINK OF OTHERS?

But wait...Superflex® Strategies can help:

LEARN what items Brain Eater uses to distract you and try to notice when your brain is getting distracted; tell yourself to "stop" and focus on what is being said. When you notice that your brain is distracted with an item in front of you, you can:

- *Move the item out of the way so you don't see it*
- *Move your body so that you don't see it*
- *Ask to be moved from your spot so that you can focus*

LEARN about Whole Body Listening and how your whole body (eyes, ears, hands, feet, etc.) listens by being quiet when others are talking.

- *Use a fidget (like a rubber chicken) to keep your whole body calm and focused. Keep the fidget out of sight so that you don't get distracted with that, too. The Brain Eater would love that!*

CAN YOU THINK OF OTHERS?

Is this an **Unthinkable** that gets into your brain?

What is a *Superflexible strategy* that you can use if you notice this Unthinkable in your brain plotting against your *Superflex*?

63

Going on a distracter hunt...

In order to defeat Brain Eater, you have to be aware of his "bait" and what he likes to use to get you distracted. Go through your house and write down items that Brain Eater tries to distract your brain with. Then, think about what things distract you at school in your classroom. Write the words in the bubble below.

Thoughts or items that distract me at school:

Thoughts or items that distract me at home:

Can you use a strategy (i.e., moving everything off your desk while studying) to help you defeat *Brain Eater?*

Lesson 8 : One More Honorable Mention... Brain Eater!

Superflex®: A Superhero Social Thinking Curriculum
Think Social Publishing, Inc. ©2008 www.socialthinking.com

Lesson #9
Levels to Becoming the Ultimate Social Thinking Superhero, Superflex

Purpose: This lesson was developed to help the students understand the process of changing their behavior. This lesson will help the children to understand that there is a learning process to becoming their ultimate Superflex®. Like many of the superheroes that we have come to know and love, they have stumbled across their powers and had to figure out how to fine-tune and master their skills. Our Superflex students are similar in that they have to be explicitly taught about their social difficulties and be taught strategies to change their behavior. As a Superflex superhero, our students are all learning about their strengths and weaknesses and how to use their "thinking" powers (strategies) more effectively. By representing the learning in levels, the students can see that this is a process, and there is a period where they work and need to take assistance from others.

This lesson was also initially developed to help students feel more comfortable and more willing to take direction from their parents, teachers, and educators when cues or prompts were given to help them identify their behavior or when an "unthinkable" moment was taking place. This lesson will also allow for a discussion on how the other students in the group can provide helpful and positive cues to their group members instead of pointing out what they are doing wrong.

Vocabulary:

Superhero Support Team: Family, caregivers, and students that are helping to positively support the child.

Levels To Becoming The Ultimate Superhero

Goals:

- The student will be able to identify the two levels involved in becoming a Superflex superhero and define the difference between each level with ___% accuracy.
- On a worksheet, the student will be able to identify three members on their Superhero support team and a cue that each person may use to help him modify his behavior with ___% accuracy.
- The student will be able to take redirection without difficulty from members of their Superhero support team with ___% accuracy.

What you need to do before the lesson:

✓ Identify a few sections from your selected movie and have the movie cued up and ready to go.

✓ Have capes and **flexible thinking*** brains ready!

Materials:

The Incredibles or Sky High movie

Comic books (see Appendix A)

Handout, Lesson #9

Funwork, Lesson #9

Capes

Flexible-thinking brains

*Refer to pages 15-17 for definition.

Teacher Review-Superflex Training Session #9:

1. Review their homework and let them share their results with the group.

2. Explain to the students that today they will be exploring the levels to becoming the ultimate Superhero. Explain that Superheroes have to work at learning and fine-tuning their powers. Superheroes do not generally do this alone but get help from others around them to become the "ultimate" Superhero. Explain that as Superflex Superheroes, they must also go through this process.

3. Show them the handout of Levels To Becoming The Ultimate Superhero (or draw this up on the board) and explain to them how all of the Superheroes they listed had to learn and start at Level 2 and work their way up to Level 1.
   a. The group can provide examples of Superheroes working to perfect their powers.
   b. Write the names of the Superheroes mentioned and connect them to Level 1.

4. As Superflex students-in-training at the academy, they are starting at Level 2 because they are learning about their skills and strategies, and once they begin mastering and consistently defeating their Unthinkables, they move into Level 1, Ultimate Superflex.

5. Watch portions of *The Incredibles* or *Sky High* movie and highlight sections where the characters are learning to control their powers, and how others around them are helping them understand their powers. This story is great because it represents the family members working together to help each other, which nicely parallels our families that we work with.

6. Give each student his Funwork, Lesson #4 handout, and ask him to identify and write his team member's names on the space provided in Level 2.

7. Make sure that on their handout they include the children in the group as members of their team. Our students are often quick to point out another's weaknesses with little regard for how this might make others feel. This "policing" can quickly agitate others in the group and ultimately make the group fall apart (I am speaking from experience). So including their group members as a part of the team allows for a nice discussion about how we are all working on skills in the group and how we can provide friendly reminders and cues. Then have each child come up with one way he would like his group mates to cue him.
   a. For example: The group is playing a game and Johnny is getting frustrated because he cannot go first. Another student can say, "Hey, Johnny, I think this is a Superflex moment; what about your strategies?" Then both of the students should be highly rewarded for taking care of each other's feelings!

66

Superflex®: A Superhero Social Thinking Curriculum
Think Social Publishing, Inc. ©2008 www.socialthinking.com

Funwork, Lesson #9:

This handout is provided to help the students begin to monitor their own behavior and provide a way for the parents to indicate how they will assist their child in calling on his or her Superflex!

    a.   For the older student (ages 8-10), suggest that the parents and child work together to come up with a cue that the parents can use when an Unthinkable moment is occurring. For some students, this allows them to feel like they have some control and say in how they are being assisted.

    b.   For example: "Mom will remind me by tapping my shoulder and telling me that Rock Brain is lurking."

Also ask the families to take a trip to their local bookstore to research and purchase a comic book that shows an example of a Superhero mastering his or her powers or receiving help from others. Have the child bring in the book for his next session.

Superflex®: A Superhero Social Thinking Curriculum
Think Social Publishing, Inc. ©2008 www.socialthinking.com

LEVELS TO BECOMING THE ULTIMATE SUPERFLEX®!

Superflex superheroes did not perfect their skills overnight. Thinking about others and making good choices are all things they had to practice, too. They quickly realized being *superflexible* takes a lot of hard work and dedication and, just like you, they had to call on their supporters to give them guidance and help to remember what strategies they can use to defeat **Unthinkables®** when they are invading.

The same is true for you as you work on becoming the ultimate superhero *Superflex*, and making great social choices. You will have to work on recognizing the **Unthinkables** and then making good choices and using your strategies to help yourself. This is not easy!

As you work to master *superflexible* thinking, your supporters will be there to help you along the way. This is nothing to be ashamed of or resist because it is all a learning process.

Take a look below to better understand the levels of becoming the ultimate Social Thinking superhero, *Superflex*. What level are you on?

LEVEL 1:
THE ULTIMATE SOCIAL THINKING SUPERHERO, SUPERFLEX!

*Able to recognize social thinking moments most of the time and use strategies to defeat **Unthinkable** without help from others.*

LEVEL 2: LEARNING LEVEL
LEARNING ABOUT YOUR SOCIAL THINKING POWERS AND HOW TO USE THEM!

*You are learning to recognize **Unthinkables** that invade your brain and how to defeat them with strategies. At this level, since you are still learning, your **Superhero Support Team** may help you recognize when an **Unthinkable** is lurking or to remember your strategies.*

68

My Path To Becoming the *Ultimate* Social Thinking® Superhero!

This week, tell all your supporters that you will need their help and reminders as you work to become the ultimate Social Thinking Superhero, *Superflex®*.

Use this sheet to keep track of how everyone is doing at helping you reach your goal. Put this sheet on your refrigerator as a reminder and bring it back to show what you and your team decided.

LEVEL 1:
THE ULTIMATE SOCIAL THINKING SUPERHERO, SUPERFLEX!

Able to recognize social thinking moments most of the time and use strategies to defeat **Unthinkable** *without help from others.*

LEVEL 2: LEARNING LEVEL
LEARNING ABOUT YOUR SOCIAL THINKING POWERS AND HOW TO USE THEM!

Show how you did your part to help your Superflex: Put a tally mark each time you used Superflex Strategies this week.

Parent's Tally: _____   Aide's Tally: _____

Cue: _____   Cue: _____

Teacher's Tally: _____   Group Member's Tally: _____

Cue: _____   Cue: _____

69

Superflex®: A Superhero Social Thinking Curriculum
Think Social Publishing, Inc. ©2008 www.socialthinking.com

Lesson #10

Putting your Superflexible Strategies to Work!

Materials:

Capes

Defeat Sheet handout

Video recording device and T.V.

Unthinkables cards from Appendix B, printed and cut apart

GAMES! GAMES! GAMES! (board games or card games). You will want to have quite a few motivating choices for the children so they have to work harder at finding a game they can all agree to play.

Handout, Lesson #10

Funwork, Lesson #10

Purpose: To address generalization skills by increasing the student's self-monitoring and regulating skills during structured and non-structured tasks through use of a positive visual system.

Vocabulary:

Defeat Sheet: Handout used to monitor when the student is using a Superflex® strategy in order to keep the Unthinkable out of his brain.

Goals:

☆ During structured tasks, the student will demonstrate ability to self-monitor his identified behavior (Unthinkable), using a visual tracking form, decreasing behavior by ___% of the time.

What you need to do before the lesson:

✓ Prepare Defeat Sheets: laminate and use Velcro strips to hold the characters on the page.

✓ Get the capes and flexible-thinking brains ready!

Teacher Review-Superflex Training Session #10

1. Pass out each child's Team Leader Unthinkable card, or, if appropriate, a more pertinent Unthinkable card that the student is working on. Have each child identify some of the powers of this character as well as what strategies will defeat him.

2. Introduce the Defeat Sheet handout and read the directions at the top. (Velcro can be used to stick the Superflex and the Unthinkable onto the sheet.) Let the students place their Unthinkable card at the bottom of the page. Help each child determine what strategy he will try to use while playing games with the other group members. Place Superflex at the top of the column.

3. Explain to the students that each time they are able to defeat their Unthinkable, Superflex moves one level closer to the bottom. If they use their Superflexible strategies and Superflex reaches the bottom before the end of the activity, then they have successfully defeated their Unthinkable!

4. Tell the students that it is time to play some games so they can practice defeating their Unthinkables and keeping them out of the room. Let the children put on their capes (if they like), grab their flexible brains and find one game that everyone would like to play.

5. Begin videotaping this activity to play at the end of the session.
   As the children play the game together, the children and educator can identify the Superflexible moments each child is having and move their Superflex character one level closer to the bottom. Your students will be at varying levels of self-awareness, and it will be important for the

educator to provide greater support if their self awareness skills are still emerging.

6.   If time permits, have the group watch their video to see how they performed. Discuss how the game went, how everyone felt playing the game, and whether they would like to play again.

7.   Pass out Superflex Awards!!

Funwork, Lesson #10:

Have the children take home the Defeat Sheet handout and monitor their skills while playing another game with Mom or Dad. Make sure to have the parents begin the activity by deciding what game the family will play. Encourage the children to bring in their Defeat Sheet each week to check in and share how they are doing at home or school with their strategies.

If time permits, the children may enjoy demonstrating what the game might look like if their Unthinkables were in their brains.

Superflex®: A Superhero Social Thinking Curriculum
Think Social Publishing, Inc. ©2008 www.socialthinking.com

THE DEFEAT SHEET!

Let's practice defeating one of your **Unthinkables®**! Your goal is to move *Superflex®* down to the bottom of your column. You can move *Superflex* down a level by using a strategy to defeat your **Unthinkable** when he pops up in group. If you can take *Superflex* to the bottom level you have successfully defeated your **Unthinkable** for today and you may turn over that **Unthinkable** Card. Good luck!

Name: _____	Name: _____	Name: _____
Attempting to defeat:	Attempting to defeat:	Attempting to defeat:
Strategy:	Strategy:	Strategy:
Pow! You did it!!	**Pow!** You did it!!	**Pow!** You did it!!
Place **Unthinkable** Here	Place **Unthinkable** Here	Place **Unthinkable** Here

Lesson 10 : Putting Your Superflexible Strategies to Work!

DEFEAT SHEET!

Defeating your Unthinkables® one at a time!

Keep working at it! You are doing great at defeating your **Unthinkable** team leaders. Practice defeating your **Unthinkable** at home using your Defeat Sheet. As a family, identify an **Unthinkable** and help your son or daughter use his or her strategies to move *Superflex*® to the bottom of the Defeat Sheet. Remember to bring in your sheet to show everyone how you did!

Attempting to defeat:

Strategy:

Pow!

You did it!!

Place **Unthinkable** Here

Superflex®: A Superhero Social Thinking Curriculum
Think Social Publishing, Inc. ©2008 www.socialthinking.com

Lesson #11
Practice...
Practice...
Practice...

Materials:
....

Poster board or butcher paper

Four game pieces

Dice

Superflex and Unthinkables cards from Appendix B, printed and cut apart

Defeat Sheet handout

Video recording device and T.V.

Funwork, Lesson #11

Purpose: To provide additional activities that can be used to allow the students to monitor their behaviors and defeat their Unthinkables® in a structured session.

Vocabulary:

Superflex
Superflex strategies
Team of Unthinkables

Goals:

✿   During structured tasks, the student will demonstrate ability to self-monitor his identified behavior (Unthinkable), using a visual tracking form, decreasing behavior by ___% of the time.

What you need to do before the lesson:

✓   If working with younger children, prepare a game board ahead of time.

✓   Get those capes and flexible-thinking brains ready!

Teacher Review-Superflex® Training Session #11:

For younger children, it would be best to have a game already created for them to play. The game can be very simple.

1.   Using the Defeat Sheet, work with the group to identify the Unthinkable that they will work on defeating today during the session.
2.   Begin monitoring each child's behavior on the Defeat Sheet and provide positive reinforcement when appropriate.
3.   Make a simple game board pattern on poster board. The object of the game is to defeat all the Unthinkables in Superflex's path to make it to the finish line.
4.   Place the Unthinkables and strategy cards in one pile, face down.
5.   Let the children generate three special spots on the game board that would allow someone to move ahead. For example: A Superflex Square which would allow a child to move ahead three spots if he could share a recent Superflexible moment.
6.   Determine the order of players.
7.   Have a child roll the dice, then pick a card from the pile. If a strategy card is drawn, he must identify which Unthinkable it is used on. If he selects an Unthinkable, he must identify a strategy that could be used to defeat the character. If the child can recall a strategy to defeat the Unthinkable, he can move the amount indicated on the dice.
8.   Take turns until someone gets to the finish spot on the board.
9.   Throughout the game, help the students monitor their behavior and move their Superflex on the Defeat Sheet.

74

For older students, the task can be more complex. These students can create their own Superflex game. Videotape the session so the kids can monitor their progress on their behavior.

1. Review the Defeat Sheet with the students and have each child come up with an Unthinkable they think may enjoy "hanging out" in their brain during the group project of making a board game.
   ⊚ You may consider starting a new Defeat Sheet when the group begins playing the game, because the Unthinkables they are trying to defeat may change given the different context of game playing.

2. Use the same game materials as listed above. Then, using a visual web, brainstorm with the group what information they will need to gather to create a game (see Diagram #2, page 76):
   a. Title
   b. Object of the game
   c. What the game board will look like
   d. How the cards will be used
   e. Any special features to the game (i.e., special bonus squares)

3. Once this information is gathered the tasks can be delegated to make the game.

4. Once the game is made allow the students to play while monitoring their identified Unthinkable.

Funwork, Lesson # 11:
Ask the families to work with their child to make their own version of a Superflex game. They can use the Defeat Sheets to monitor their skills while working with the family on this project and while playing the actual game.

Diagram #2

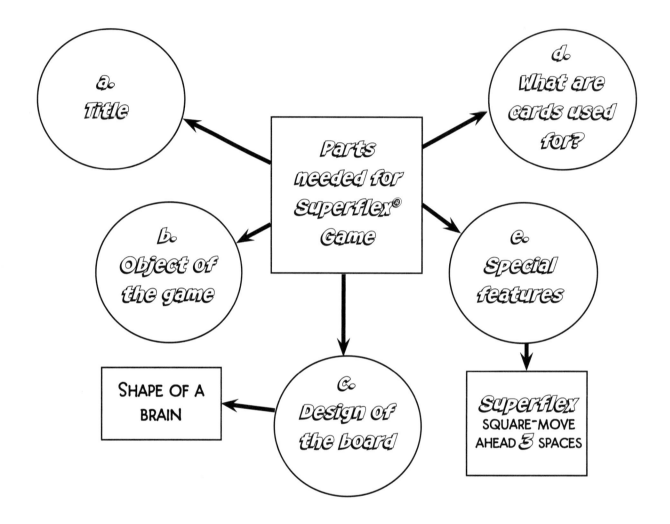

DEFEAT SHEET!

Work with your family to create another **Superflex**® game. Remember that the **Unthinkables**® live for these situations when you have to work with others or play games so BE CAREFUL! Bring your game in next week to show the group!

Attempting to defeat:

Strategy:

POW!
You did it!!

Place **Unthinkable** Here

77

Lesson #12
Superflex Academy
Graduation Party

Materials:

Defeat Sheet Handout

Handout, Lesson #12

Funwork, Lesson #12

Superflex and Unthinkables cards from Appendix B, printed and cut apart

Purpose: To reward the Superflex® Academy® students for weeks of hard work! Also, to give them another enriched opportunity to work on defeating their Unthinkables and celebrating their Superflex accomplishments. We all know party planning requires maximum perspective-taking, and the students will be put to the test with this activity.

Vocabulary:

Superflex
Superflex strategies
Team of Unthinkables
Flexible thinking*

Goals:

✿ The student will identify an appropriate Unthinkable to monitor during a party planning activity with ___% accuracy.
✿ The student will monitor and use a strategy to defeat the identified Unthinkable with ___% accuracy.
✿ The student, during a structured activity and using a visual tool, will defeat an identified Unthinkable ___% of the time.

Teacher Review-Superflex Training Session #12:

1. Review homework and let the children share the Superflex games that they created. These games can be brought back to be played at their Superflex party.
2. Explain that before graduation from the Academy, the students usually plan a Superhero Party to celebrate and reward themselves for all their hard work.
3. However, assure your students that as much fun as that sounds, the Team of Unthinkables sees it as another opportunity to defeat Superflex. Maybe the Unthinkables find that students are having so much fun planning and having a party they let their guard down, making the students an easy target!
4. Ask the students whether they still think they should have the party? After they excitedly agree to have the party, show them the Defeat Sheet and work with them to identify the most appropriate Unthinkable; place on the Defeat Sheet.
5. Plan the party with the students using Handout, Lesson #12, and monitoring their **Superflexible thinking***!

Funwork, Lesson #12:

This assignment is used to help the students see the task of planning a party to its completion. Many of our students, once they leave the session, forget that they have to bring anything to the party; then the responsibility lies with the parents. Encourage the parents to sit and plan out tasks for the week. Of course, the complexity of this task will depend on their age. For young children, their task may involve simply going with Mom or Dad to the store to find the item.

78

Superflex®: A Superhero Social Thinking Curriculum
Think Social Publishing, Inc. ©2008 www.socialthinking.com

Superflex® Party!

CONGRATULATIONS, STUDENTS! You are close to graduating from the Academy and what better way to celebrate than to have a party? Now, like any party there must be food and games! However, to honor our hero Superflex, all the food that is brought to the party must be "Flexible" (i.e., gummy snacks or cheese sticks) or relate to Superheroes in some way. The games or activities at the party must also involve a Superhero theme (i.e., Pin the Brain on the Unthinkable, make a Superflex Mask) or involve flexible thinking.

Take some time to plan out the party details with your classmates and remember to think about others.

Name	Activity	Items needed for Activity	Snack

Superflex®: A Superhero Social Thinking Curriculum
Think Social Publishing, Inc. ©2008 www.socialthinking.com

Party Planning

Now that you know what you are bringing to the party next week, you still have to make sure you get all the items you need. This may involve some flexible thinking. The trick is not to wait until the last minute! To help you plan, fill out the handout below with one of your parents and then check off each item on your list as you do it!

What do you need to take to the party?	What do you need to do to get this item(s)?	What day will I do this?	Put a check if done.
SODA	ASK MOM TO TAKE ME TO THE STORE ON MONDAY	TUESDAY	✓

🖐 DON'T FORGET TO PUT ALL YOUR ITEMS IN A BAG AND PUT IT IN A PLACE SO YOU DON'T FORGET THEM. MAYBE THE BAG CAN BE LEFT IN YOUR PARENT'S CAR?

80

Superflex®: A Superhero Social Thinking Curriculum
Think Social Publishing, Inc. ©2008 www.socialthinking.com

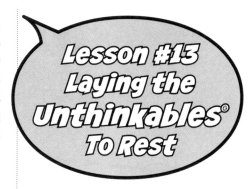

Lesson #13
Laying the Unthinkables® To Rest

Purpose: As the students improve in their ability to monitor their behavior, it will be important to recognize their accomplishments. The purpose of this activity is to reinforce generalization of the skills and strategies they have implemented to increase their social thinking. The "Laid To Rest" handout is made so that it can be modified depending on the setting or activity. The child could have a "Laid To Rest" sheet specifically for the park or recess. Selecting a specific context such as the park will allow the student to give direct attention to his behavior within that setting, which will also promote success.

 This lesson could take place during the Superflex® Party.

Vocabulary:

Superflex
Superflex strategy
Laid to Rest: Unthinkable is retired from the list once a student has successfully defeated one Unthinkable, three consecutive sessions.

Goal:

☆ The student will successfully defeat a determined Unthinkable using a Superflexible Strategy in three consecutive treatment sessions with ___% accuracy.

☆ Within a social context at school or home, the student will successfully defeat a determined Unthinkable using a Superflexible Strategy in three consecutive times with ___% accuracy

What you need to do before the lesson:

✓ Print out photos (taken during Lesson #4) of your Superflex students and attach to the Laid To Rest sheet.

✓ The Laid To Rest sheet can be replicated on a large piece of butcher paper or poster board and displayed in the treatment room for all to see, or each child could have his own Laid To Rest sheet dedicated to his specific Unthinkables. This is up to you!

✓ If hanging a larger version of the Laid To Rest sheet on butcher or poster paper, make sure to separate the photos to allow for enough space to place their Unthinkables next to their pictures.

Teacher Review-Superflex Training Lesson #13:

1. Introduce the Laid To Rest sheet to the group and share with the group the amazing accomplishments you have witnessed from your group of Superflex students.
2. Explain that their hard work is beginning to pay off as you realize: they

Materials:

Handout/Funwork, Lesson #13

Unthinkables cards from Appendix B, cut out

Individual photos of your Superflex students

Superflex cape

Poster boards or butcher paper (if desired)

81

Superflex®: A Superhero Social Thinking Curriculum
Think Social Publishing, Inc. ©2008 www.socialthinking.com

Note: At this point, only some or one of the children may qualify for laying one of their Unthinkables to rest. Stress to the group that it is only a matter of time before their Unthinkables are laid to rest, and this display may help boost their motivation.

are working better in the group and **thinking about others*** more; others around them are feeling good; and the group is able to stay together and does not fall apart.

3. Announce who in the group has managed to keep out an Unthinkable for three or more consecutive weeks. Hand that child his Unthinkable card to hang on the Laid To Rest sheet and hand him his Superflex photo (taken during lesson #4). Let the child sign his Superflex signature on the Unthinkable card and place it on his Laid To Rest sheet or near the photo on the larger version.

4. The **Superflexible thinking*** does not stop there. Encourage the children to get their Defeat Sheet ready and determine what Unthinkables they may need to keep out of their brains during the Superflex Party.

5. Let's get the party started!

Funwork, Lesson #13:

Give the parents a copy of Handout Lesson #13. Ask that this be displayed in a location in the house where everyone can see their child's Superflex accomplishments. The handout can also be passed on to the teacher and aide (if appropriate) and they can identify a location at the child's desk, a Superflex binder or a wall in the classroom. When appropriate, the teacher can identify an Unthinkable that the child has managed to keep out of his brain in the context (i.e., classroom, recess, 4-square, etc.).

*Refer to pages 15-17 for definition.

82

Superflex®: A Superhero Social Thinking Curriculum
Think Social Publishing, Inc. ©2008 www.socialthinking.com

THE FOLLOWING UNTHINKABLES®
HAVE BEEN LAID TO REST AT

(setting)

BY... SUPERFLEX®!

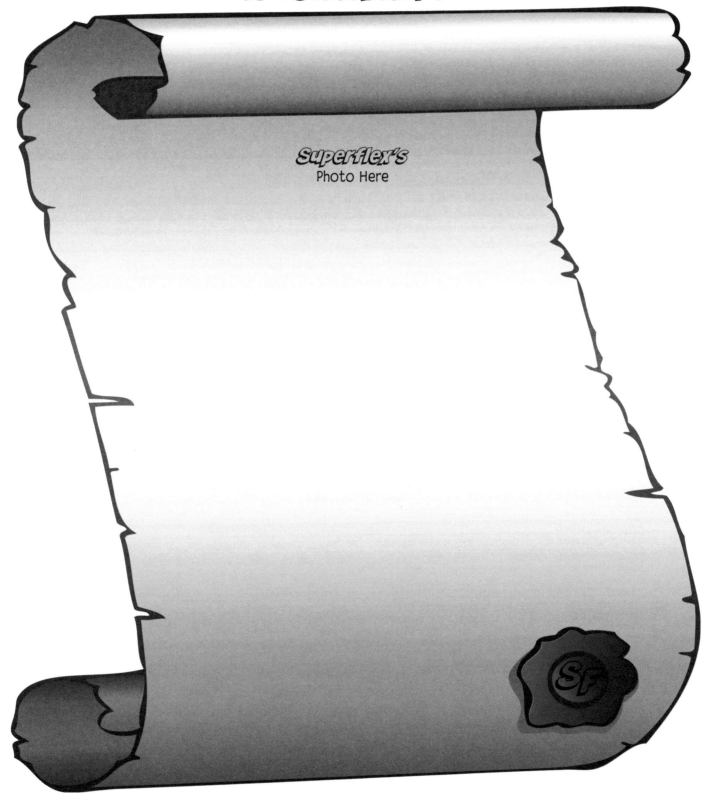

Superflex's
Photo Here

Superflex®: A Superhero Social Thinking Curriculum
Think Social Publishing, Inc. ©2008 www.socialthinking.com

Appendix A:
Books and Materials related to Superflex® Curriculum

Unthinkables®	RELATED BOOKS
Rock Brain	*Arthur's Family Vacation: An Arthur Adventure*
	Five Little Monkeys Jumping On The Bed
	It's Hard To Be Five: Learning How To Work My Control Panel
	Alexander And The Terrible, Horrible, No Good, Very Bad Day
	Monkey Do!
	If You Give A Pig A Pancake
	If You Give A Moose A Muffin
	If You Give A Mouse A Cookie
	If You Give A Pig A Party
	Miss Nelson Is Missing!
	Miss Nelson Has A Field Day
Brain Eater	*The Very Noisy Night*
Body Snatcher	*Angelina And Henry*
D.O.F. The Destroyer of Fun	*Winners Never Quit!*
	Being A Bad Sport (Help Me Be Good Series)
Un-Wonderer	*Watch Out!*
Space Invader	*Buzz, Buzz, Buzz went Bumblebee*
Glassman	*When Sophie Gets Angry...Really Really Angry*
	The Remarkable Farkle McBride
Grump Grumpaniny	*The Grouchy Lady Bug*
	Grumpy Gloria
Topic Twistermeister	*My Mouth Is A Volcano*
WasFunnyOnce	*Giggle, Giggle, Quack*
Energy Hare-y	*Five Little Monkeys Jumping On The Bed*
One-Sided Sid	*If You Give A Pig A Pancake*
	Fancy Nancy
Worry Wall	*My First Day of School*
	Franklin In The Dark
	Franklin And The Thunderstorm
	Franklin's Bad Day
	The Kissing Hand
Mean Jean/Gene	*The Recess Queen*
	Miss Nelson Is Missing!
	Miss Nelson Has A Field Day

84

Superflex®: A Superhero Social Thinking Curriculum
Think Social Publishing, Inc. ©2008 www.socialthinking.com

Books:

Ahlberg, A. (1998). *Monkey Do!* Cambridge, MA: Candle Wick Press.

Allard, H. (1977). *Miss Nelson Is Missing.* New York, NY: Houghton Mifflin Co.

Allard, H. (1985). *Miss Nelson Has A Field Day.* Boston, MA.: Houghton Mifflin Co.

Bang, M. (1999). *When Sophie Gets Angry...Really Really Angry.* New York, NY: Scholastic Inc.

Berry, J. (1985). *Being a Bad Sport.* Grolier Enterprises Corp.

Bourgeois, P. (1997). *Franklin's Bad Day.* New York, NY: Scholastic Inc.

Bourgeois, P. (1986). *Franklin in the Dark.* New York, NY: Scholastic Inc.

Bourgeois, P. (1998). *Franklin and The Thunderstorm.* New York, NY: Scholastic Inc.

Brown, M. (1993). *Arthur's Family Vacation: An Arthur Adventure.* New York, NY: Little Brown and Company.

Carle, E. (1996). *The Grouchy Ladybug.* China: Harper Collins Publisher.

Christelow, E. (1989). *Five Little Monkeys Jumping on the Bed.* New York, NY: Clarion Books.

Cook, J. (2005). *My Mouth is a Volcano.* Warrenton, VA: CTC Publishing.

Cronin, D. (2002). *Giggle, Giggle, Quack.* New York, NY: Simon and Schuster Books for Young Readers.

Curtis, J. and L. Cornell. (2004). *It's Hard To Be Five: Learning How To Work My Control Panel.* Joanna Cotler Books.

Dewdney, A. (2006) *Grumpy Gloria.* New York, NY: Viking.

Fearnley, J. (2004) *Watch Out!* Cambridge, MA: Candlewick Press.

Hallinan, P.K. (1987). *My First Day of School.* New York, NY: Ideals Publishing Corp.

Hamm, M. (2004)*Winners Never Quit!* New York, NY: Harper Collins.

Hendry, D. (1999) *The Very Noisy Night.* New York, NY: Dalton Children's Books.

Holabird, K. (2002). *Angelina and Henry.* Middleton, Wisconsin: Pleasant Company Publications.

Lithgow, J. (2000). *The Remarkable Farkle McBride.* New York, NY: Simon & Schuster Books for Young Readers.

Numeroff, L. (1998). *If You Give A Pig A Pancake.* New York, NY:Laura Geringer Pub.

Numeroff, L. (1991). *If You Give A Moose A Muffin.* New York, NY:Laura Geringer Pub.

Numeroff, L. (1985). *If You Give A Mouse A Cookie.* New York, NY:Laura Geringer Pub.

Numeroff, L. (2005). *If You Give A Pig A Party.* New York, NY:Laura Geringer Pub.

O'Connor, J. (2005). *Fancy Nancy.* New York, NY: Harper Collins Children's Books.

O'Neill, A. (2002). *The Recess Queen.* New York, NY: Scholastic Press. .

Penn, A. (1993). *The Kissing Hand.* Terre Haute, IN: Tanglewood Press.

Viorst, J. (1987). *Alexander and the Terrible, Horrible, No Good, Very Bad Day.* New York, NY: Aladdin Publishing.

West, C. (1996). *Buzz, Buzz, Buzz went Bumblebee.* Cambridge, Mass: Candlewick Press.

Movies

Sky High, Disney. 2005.
The Incredibles, Pixar. 2004.

Games:

Operation by Hasbro
Operation Brain Surgery by Hasbro

Products:

Gelatin Brain Mold, www.Amazon.com
Klutz *Superhero Starter Kit.* Klutz: Palo Alto, CA. 2006.

Appendix B

Definitions – *Superflex®* and *Team of Unthinkables* Cards

Superhero	Superflex's strengths
 *Superflex®*	Our hero! Totally flexible, trying to figure out people's wants and needs to keep other people calm while also getting his turn to play and to speak as well. Superflex is a great problem-solver and can think of many different solutions to one problem. (Note: in our storybook and curriculum, the Superflex you read about is Aiden's Superflex. Your Superflex looks like you, mine looks like me, etc. Find a fun **Superflex is Me** handout at the end of the book to draw your own Superflex!)

Team of Unthinkables	The "powers" they have over our brains	*Superflex Strategies* to solve the problem and defeat the Unthinkable
 Rock Brain	He will get the person to do only what he wants to do and will not let him negotiate with other people. The person is not a good problem-solver and tries one solution that's not working over and over again. This person may be very rule bound and rigid in his thinking, only seeing one way to a situation.	Notice that what you are doing is not working and try another way to solve the same problem. Take a deep breath and remember that being part of a group means that you cannot always do it your way or make the decisions you want. Self talk: "Not a problem, I will get to do this later or another time…" Ask yourself, "What is their plan?" And then try to match their plan.
 Brain Eater	He makes it hard for the person to focus on what he is doing or focus on others during interactions (roll his brain away). The person may get easily distracted with his own thoughts or things around him.	Turn your body and eyes away from what is distracting you and think about the person talking. Use a fidget so that it keeps your body busy but your brain focused on the group. Try to notice when your brain is thinking about something else and get it to refocus on the group.

86

Superflex®: A Superhero Social Thinking Curriculum
Think Social Publishing, Inc. ©2008 www.socialthinking.com

Team of Unthinkables	The "powers" they have over our brains	Superflex Strategies to solve the problem and defeat the Unthinkable
Body Snatcher 	He gets the person to wander away from others (roll his body away) and not stay with the group or person he is with. May also get the person to turn his body away from the group, not realizing the message he is sending to others.	Use your eyes to think about where your group is or who is talking to you, and find the group! <hr> Self-talk: "Where should my body be?" <hr> Point your shoulders to the group.
D.O.F. The Destroyer of Fun 	This character often pops up during games or activities involving competition. The person becomes overly competitive and insists on going first, playing only what he wants to play, and does not think about compromising or about how he makes others feel.	Self-talk: "If I am a "Just Me" player, then my friends will not have a good time." <hr> Self-Talk: "Tiny problem. I will still get a turn or may win another time."
Un-Wonderer 	He stops the person from showing interest (social wondering) in others or thinking about what others may want to do. <hr> The person may not ask a lot of questions about others or add his ideas to what they are playing.	Look at the person who is talking to let him know that you are thinking about him and what he is saying. <hr> Listen to the topic and then ask a "social wonder" question of your friend. <hr> Create a people-file in your brain to call on later to ask questions. <hr> Remember the Wh-question words and use them to think of questions for your friends.
Space Invader 	This character makes the person's body move into other people's personal space when others are not expecting it or do not want this. He does not realize how uncomfortable this makes others feel.	Use one-arm rule to determine if you are standing too close to someone. <hr> Think about what your body looks like in the group. Are you making others have good thoughts or weird thoughts? If you are making others have weird thoughts, adjust your body.

87

Team of Unthinkables	The "powers" they have over our brains	*Superflex Strategies* to solve the problem and defeat the Unthinkable
Glassman 	Lets a person be flexible to some extent, but then all of a sudden he just breaks. He doesn't melt down slowly; he quickly starts getting very upset often over "tiny" problems. Glassman usually thinks things aren't "fair."	Identify the size of the problem (1-10) and what would be an expected reaction to match the size of the problem. Self-Talk: "I am starting to get mad. I need to move away and take a break or tighten all of the muscles in my body and then relax them.
Grump Grumpaning 	Makes the person think the worst or feel like people are always unkind. He ends up believing it even when people are trying to be nice. He may also see everything as negative or bad and does not see how his emotion spreads and makes everyone feel unhappy.	Think about how the person treats you. Is he friendly or mean to you? If this person is friendly to me then he is not being mean to me. Self talk: "I am being negative. What could be a positive way to think about it?"
Topic Twistermeister 	This character gets the person to twist the topic around to what he wants to talk about and goes off on tangents when talking to others. This person may then go on and on about topics he wants to talk about, not realizing that others may be bored or disinterested in what he is talking about.	Check-in with those around you. Does it look like they are interested in what you are saying? If not, ask a question about what they might want to talk about. Turn off your "Me" button and try to think only about the other person by asking him questions.
WasFunnyOnce 	This person will attempt to use a lot of humor to be funny. However, he does not realize that humor wears out pretty quickly or at times is not "funny" at all. He has trouble recognizing appropriate times for humor and may try to be funny during a discussion in a classroom or when the moment is serious and not funny or silly. Some people may get so silly, that the other children become silly also making the group fall apart. This is called getting caught up in the "silly tornado."	Self-talk: "Is now a silly moment or a serious moment?" If a serious moment, then this is not a good time to crack a joke or say something that I think is funny. Use the one-time-rule: only say the word or joke once and then move on so that the joke does not get boring for others.

Appendix B:Definitions — Superflex® and Team of Unthinkables Cards

Superflex®: A Superhero Social Thinking Curriculum
Think Social Publishing, Inc. ©2008 www.socialthinking.com

Team of Unthinkables	The "powers" they have over our brains	*Superflex Strategies* to solve the problem and defeat the Unthinkable
Energy Hare-y 	This character gives the person so much energy so that he is constantly fidgeting or moving around, and he doesn't think about what the people around him needs or how others are feeling around them. Sometimes, Energy Hare-y and WasFunnyOnce work together, which can quickly make the group fall apart.	When others are talking, use Whole Body Listening (keep your whole body quiet). Check in with your eyes and see how the rest of the group is acting. Try to match how calm the other kids are with their bodies. Take a few deep breaths to calm your body.
One-Sided Sid 	This character gets the person to talk about his own set of topics or his own plan. Even when someone else brings up his interests, he just talks about his own interests. He may interrupt to talk about what is on his mind, not seeing that someone may have another plan.	Open your people-file and think about what you know about the person. Ask questions to find out more about him and his experiences or interests. Think with your eyes to figure out what the person's plan is. If he looks busy, save your question for another time. Look for clues that others are not interested: looking away, bored look, trying to change the topic.
Worry Wall 	He makes the person worry or feel nervous so much about the people around him or the social situations that he or she "hits a wall" and stops being able to talk at all to the people nearby.	Close your eyes, take a deep breath, and let it out slowly. Continue to do this until your body feels relaxed. Find a thought that can change how you are feeling. "Johnny is nice; he will help me with this."
Mean Jean/Gene 	This person becomes just plain mean to other people. He or she insults or criticizes others. He or she may take things away from them, be very bossy, or hog all the attention when others are trying to talk.	Think about what you are going to say before you say it. Self-talk: "Will this hurt my friend's feelings?" Keep bragging, bossy, or hurtful thoughts in our brains.

89

Superflex®: A Superhero Social Thinking Curriculum
Think Social Publishing, Inc. ©2008 www.socialthinking.com

1. Superflexible Behavior: Thinking about others (what someone else is thinking and feeling) and the expected behaviors.

Mom is not being very nice but if I say that to her, it will hurt her feelings.

"Okay, mom."

"You are mean!"

Superflexible Moment: A. Child keeps his hurtful thoughts in his brain and says, "Okay" when his mother asks him to come in for dinner.

Superflexible Strategy: Child thinks about how his words may hurt his mom's feelings.

Rock Brain Moment: B. Child blurts out that his mom is mean and never lets him play with his friends, and he continues to play.

2. Superflexible Behavior: Being able to STOP what you are doing and follow what others are asking you to do.

"Time to clean up."

I don't want to make everyone late. I will get to play later.

This is too fun to stop.

Superflexible Moment: A. Child picks up his blocks as soon as he hears the teacher say, "It is time to clean up."

Superflexible Strategy: Child thinks about how others may be late to lunch, how frustrated his teacher may feel if he continues to play and that he may get to play blocks tomorrow.

Rock Brain Moment: B. Child continues to play even though he knows it is time to go to lunch.

91

3. Superflexible Behavior: During play, shift and adjust thinking to match what others are thinking; helping you stay connected.

I like my factories, but I can play that later.

"I can make a cage for the lions."

"Hey, you build building #2 for my factory."

Superflexible Moment: A. The children are creating a zoo with blocks. One child sees that one boy is making cages for the tigers. He replies, "I can make the cage for the lions."

Superflexible Strategy: Child "thinks with his eyes" to figure out the plan and then adds his thoughts.

Another Superflexible Strategy: Child thinks to himself, "I really like my factories but I need to think about what others want to play. I can build my factories later."

Rock Brain Moment: B. The child is very interested in factories and insists that the others build a part to his factory.

4. Superflexible Behavior: Shifting and adjusting our thinking to keep others sharing their ideas and having a good time.

"I just saw the new Superflex movie."

I wonder what his favorite part was?

"What was your favorite part?"

CARS!

"Have you seen the Cars movie?"

Superflexible Moment: A. Child listens to what the other students are talking about and asks another child a question related to the topic.

Superflexible Strategy: Child listens with his whole body to figure out the topic and then adds a thought or asks a question (social wondering).

Rock Brain Moments: B. Child continues to bring up his favorite topic of cars even though the group is trying to talk about something different.

5. Superflexible Behavior: Being able to stop and look at a problem and the variety of choices that one can use to solve it.

Superflexible Moment: A. Child goes over to the boy and asks if he can take a turn, and then waits patiently.

Superflexible Strategy: Child thinks about the size of the problem (tiny or earthquake size) and if he asks and waits for his turn, he will get to ride the bike.

Rock Brain Moment: B. Child goes over and pulls on the bike while yelling that he wants to take a turn.

6. Superflexible Behavior: Thinking about what is expected depending on where you are, what you are doing and who is there.

Superflexible Moment: A. People are in the waiting room reading books and magazines, so the child picks up a book and quietly sits down.

Superflexible Strategy: Child thinks with his eyes to figure out what others are doing and what is expected so that he can match the behavior of the other people.

Rock Brain Moment: B. Child is in a waiting room loudly bouncing his ball and asking others to join him.

Appendix E

Additional Superflex® and Unthinkable Handouts

NOTE: Handouts for Rock Brain, Brain Eater, and D.O.F.
are embedded in the Lessons, and can be found
on pages 33, 59, and 63.

Superflex® is ME!

You may have heard of superheroes who have the power to fly, freeze, orbecome invisible. But have you heard about Superflex®? Superflex is one of the greatest superheroes of all time! Superflex's super powers help us think about others!

Here's the cool thing... We each can develop our own Superflex by learning about our own superflexible thinking and strategies. It takes many years to develop our own strong Superflex, but this is where we begin learning - by imagining our own superflexible self! I will develop the powers to be my own Superflex. I have a hero inside me, willing and able to learn!

You begin by first learning to think about others and what is happening around you. As you get older, your Superflex helps you find and use the right strategies to be a flexible thinker and problem solver and helps you be part of the group plan.

Your Superflex helps you stay calm and focused during difficult moments! Your Superflex gives you many powers.

Being a Superflex is not always easy... All of these super powers take learning, practice and work. Together with your team (your family, teachers, and friends) you can learn more about and use your superflexible thinking powers!

Superflex® is ME!

Here are 3 things I can do well with my superflexible thinking:

1. _____

2. _____

3. _____

Superflex's Home Page

BORN: (AIDEN'S SUPERFLEX)
August 17, 2000

PLACE OF BIRTH:
Social Town, USA

NICKNAME:
Flexie (but only called this by his mom)

 **Powers:**

Totally flexible thinker! This means he can prevent his brain from getting stuck on thinking about something one way-his way!

Helps citizens think about how to act and behave to keep others feeling good.

He is a great problem solver and can think of many different solutions to one problem.

Helps a citizen to recognize when an Unthinkable might be getting into their brain and can quickly come up with a Superflex strategy to defeat the character.

MINI BIOGRAPHY:
Superflex© quickly became the talk of Social Town when he realized he had special powers to help citizens change their thinking to defeat the always looming Team of Unthinkables. Since that day, he has been the hero of this town.

LITTLE KNOWN FACTS ABOUT SUPERFLEX:
FAVORITE FOODS: Anything chewy and flexible...pasta is his favorite!
CAPE SIZE: Medium
FLIGHT SPEED: 100 mph when in pursuit of an Unthinkable
FAVORITE ENERGY FOODS: Superflex Cereal with lots of fruit

ACCOMPLISHMENTS:
- In 2007, he received the Social Town Medal for great service to his community.
- In 2007 he created the Superflex Academy to teach the children of Social Town how to be their own superhero.

TRIVIA:
- *What is the name of his dog?* Bark
- *How many Superflex Strategy Brains can he carry in his cape at one time?* 50
- *What is his favorite color?* Blue
- *What is his favorite video game?* Superflex Soccer
- *What does he like to read?* Superhero Comic Books
- *What does he like to do when he is not trying to defeat the Unthinkables?* Play fetch with his dog, Bark

Quotes From **Citizens of Social Town**

" *People here are so thoughtful and friendly...living here makes me feel great about myself!*"

Sally, baker at Social Town Bakery

" *Superflex has helped me make Social Town a better place!*"

Mayor of Social Town

(Make your own personalized Superflex Home Page!)

Does your brain often prevent you from **showing interest** *(social wondering) in others or considering what others may want to do based on their interests?*

Then you may be getting a visit from **the Un-Wonderer!**

The **Un-Wonderer** is pretty quiet and can sneak in when you least expect it. Take a look below for some clues to help you spot the Un-Wonderer:

🤚 He stops the citizen from showing interest in others (asking someone questions about their interests).

🤚 He stops the citizen from thinking about what others may want to do based on their interests.

No problem... *Superflex®* and the **Un-Wonderer** have battled before so take a look below for some ways to defeat this lastest Unthinkable.

👍 **Look at the person** who is talking to let him know that you are thinking about him and what he is saying.

👍 **Listen to the topic** and then ask a "social wonder" question to your friend.

👍 **Create a people-file** in your brain on this person so that you can pull up that information later when you are talking to him.

👍 **Remember the Wh-question words** (what, where, who, when which and why) and use these words to ask others questions about what they may want to talk about.

99

Superflex®: A Superhero Social Thinking Curriculum
Think Social Publishing, Inc. ©2008 www.socialthinking.com

A *NEW VILLAIN* HAS MADE HIS WAY TO EARTH. HIS NAME IS:

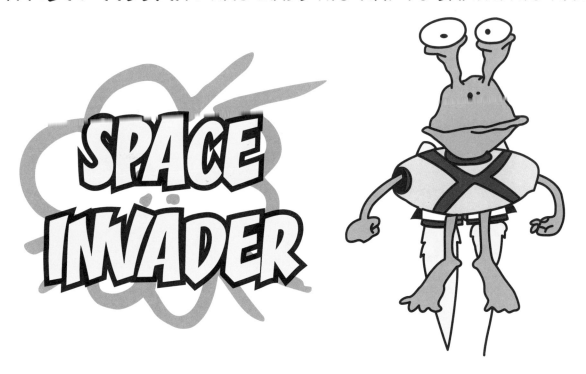

He is trying to make others break the rule of personal space so that they can make not-so-good impressions on others.

Well, *Superflex*® will have none of that! He is working to help the citizens protect themselves from the Space Invader by helping them to remember:

- 👍 The one-arm rule
- 👍 Doing the check-in and reading the clues
- 👍 Putting on the brakes and stopping themselves from getting too close to someone else

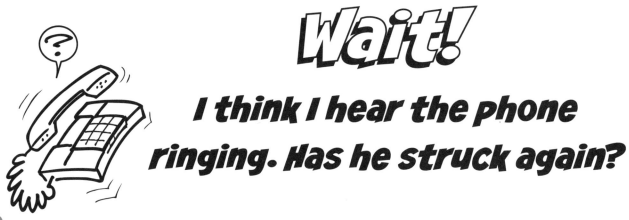

Wait!
I think I hear the phone ringing. Has he struck again?

100

Superflex®: A Superhero Social Thinking Curriculum
Think Social Publishing, Inc. ©2008 www.socialthinking.com

Superflex® to the rescue!!!

ARRRGGH!

Mean Jean/Gene

is one of **Superflex's** trickiest nemeses. This Unthinkable can often be disguised quite well, but not well enough for Superflex. Over the years, Superflex has developed some great strategies to use against Mean Jean/Gene. Take a look. You might even be able to come up with a few strategies yourself.

Mean Jean/Gene's Plans

1. May get you to say mean or hurtful things to others.

2. May get you to insult someone or name call.

3. May get you to grab or take things from others.

4. May get you to get easily upset about tiny problems (i.e., someone is trying to talk at the same time and you insist that you were talking first and he must stop talking).

5. May get you to quickly have a big reaction to a tiny problem and YELL at others.

6. May get you to insist that things go your way and others do what you want to do **ALL THE TIME!**

Strategies to defeat Mean Jean/Gene

Self-talk:
"Will this hurt my friend's feelings?"

Keep bragging, bossy, or hurtful thoughts in our brains.

101

WANTED

Worry Wall

Height: 1 inch
Weight: 2 pounds
Disguises: He may disguise himself as a picket fence or change the colors of his bricks so that he is not noticed.

Be on the lookout for this character. If you find him in your brain, notify *Superflex®!*

Worry Wall's powers include:
He will make the person worry or feel nervous so much about the people around him or the social situations that he or she "hits a wall" and stops being able to talk at all to the people nearby.

How *Superflex* can defeat this character:

👍 **Close your eyes,** take a deep breath, and let it out slowly. Continue to do this until your body feels relaxed.

👍 **Find a thought** that can change how you are feeling. *"Johnny is nice. He will help me with this."*

102

FLX-Channel 3 Late Breaking News

NEW UNTHINKABLE ON THE LOOSE!

Body Snatcher

Good afternoon students. *Superflex*® has just reported to us that a new **Unthinkable** is making his way into brains everywhere! Citizens are easily fooled by this **Unthinkable** and often do not notice when **Body Snatcher** makes their bodies walk away from others. When this happens, others may feel worried or confused because it is very unexpected to leave one person or a group of people.

Please read below to find out what he looks like and what other powers he can possess.

👎 He gets the person to wander away from others (roll his body away) and not stay with the group or person he is with.

👎 May also get the person to turn his body away from the group, not realizing the message he is sending to others.

IF YOU SPOT THIS CHARACTER IN YOUR BRAIN, BE CAREFUL. HE IS ARMED WITH HIS SUCTION HOSES AND CAN USE THEM WITHOUT WARNING.

IF SPOTTED, TRY SOME OF THESE STRATEGIES:

👍 **Use your eyes to think** about where your group is or who is talking to you and find the group!

👍 **Self-talk:** "Where should my body be?"

👍 **Point your shoulders** to the group.

103

Beware of glass!!!

Glassman, that is!!

One of the most common unthinkables who can make someone shatter – if he gets into his brain.

He lets a person be flexible to some extent, but then all of a sudden he just breaks. He doesn't melt down slowly; he quickly starts getting very upset, often over "tiny" problems.

Glassman usually thinks things aren't "fair."

Does this sound familiar? Do you know someone who gets invaded by Glassman? Do you think Glassman is on your team of unthinkables? If so, do not worry because Superflex can help.

Some ways that Superflex® suggests taking on Glassman:

- 👍 **Identify the size of the problem** (1-10) and what would be an expected reaction to match the size of the problem.

- 👍 **Self-Talk:** "I'm starting to get mad. I need to move away and take a break."

- 👍 When getting frustrated, **tighten** all of the muscles in my body **and** then **relax** them.

104

Hopping to a brain near you...
Energy Hare-y!

Listen up students
because *Energy Hare-y* loves to hang out at the *Superflex® Academy!*

Can you spot him?

Does he pop into your brain sometimes?

This character gives the person **so much energy** that he is constantly fidgeting or moving around, and he doesn't think about what the people around him need or how others are feeling around him. Sometimes, *Energy Hare-y* and *WasFunnyOnce* work together, which can quickly make the group fall apart.

Can you think of other places where you may notice him getting into your brain?
Why do we want to defeat him if we catch him in our brains? What can Hare-y do to a group?

Well, do not fear because *Superflex* has some ways to defeat this character. Take a look:

👍 When others are talking, use **Whole Body Listening** (keep your whole body quiet).

👍 **Check-in with your eyes** and see how the rest of the group is acting. Try to match how calm the other kids are with their bodies.

👍 **Take a few deep breaths** to calm.

👍 Can you think of any other strategies?

105

Superflex®: A Superhero Social Thinking Curriculum
Think Social Publishing, Inc. ©2008 www.socialthinking.com

On the Loose....

HAHA

WasFunnyOnce!!!!!!!!!

The power he may have over someone's brain:

- Will attempt to get the person to use a lot of humor to be funny. However, he does not realize that humor wears out pretty quickly or at times is not "funny" at all.

- Gets the person to have trouble recognizing appropriate times for humor and may try to be funny during a discussion in a classroom or when the moment is serious and not funny or silly.

- Some people may get so silly that the other children become silly also, making the group fall apart. This is called getting caught up in the "silly tornado."

How others feel when WasFunnyOnce GETS IN YOUR BRAIN...

- **ANNOYED**—because they are trying to follow the plan of the teacher or the group
- **FRUSTRATED**—because they are trying to focus on other things or their friends
- **GROSSED OUT**—and may not want to be around you or have you in a group
- **UNCOMFORTABLE**—because what you are doing is an unexpected behavior.

Luckily there are ways to defeat this character when he tries to come invade your brain...

- **Self-Talk** "Is now a silly moment or a serious moment?" If a serious moment, then this is not a good time to crack a joke or say something that I think is funny.

- Use the **one-time-rule:** only say the word or joke once and then move on so that the joke does not get boring for others.

- Use the **5 Point Silly Scale** to help you locate where you are on the scale so you can change yourself to a 1 or a 2.

106

Does your brain get stuck on topics that you are interested in?

Do you like to talk about your topics most of the time and sometimes interrupt to do it?

Does your brain get you to only think and talk about your plan?

Well, if so, you may be experiencing a visit from:

One-Sided Sid

The latest **Unthinkable** trying to plot against **Superflex®!**

If you think this character is on your team of unthinkables then you can call the **Superflex Hotline** at 435-3 or keep reading for **Superflexible Strategies** to defeat this character.

Superflexible strategies:

- 👍 **Open your friend-file** and think about what you know about the person. Ask questions to find out more about him and his experiences or interests.

- 👍 **Think with your eyes** to figure out what the person's plan is. If he looks busy, save your question for another time.

- 👍 **Look for clues** that others are not interested: looking away, bored look, trying to change the topic.

107

Superflex®: A Superhero Social Thinking Curriculum
Think Social Publishing, Inc. ©2008 www.socialthinking.com

Be on the lookout for...

Topic Twistermeister

He could be headed your way!!

He can try to take over your brain at any time and loves to try and defeat *Superflex®!!*

Look for these signs:

🔍 This character gets the person to twist the topic around to what he wants to talk about and goes off on tangents when talking to others.

🔍 Topic Twistermeister may get the person to go on and on about topics he wants to talk about, not realizing that others may be bored or disinterested in what he is talking about.

How he can be defeated by *Superflex:*

👍 **Check-in** with those around you. Does it look like they are interested in what you are saying? If not, ask a question about what they might want to talk about.

👍 **Turn off your "Me" button** and try to think only about the other person by asking him questions.

Appendix E: Additional Superflex® and Unthinkable Handouts

Superflex®: A Superhero Social Thinking Curriculum
Think Social Publishing, Inc. ©2008 www.socialthinking.com

Are You Grumpy?

Do you tend to view things as negative or bad, sometimes, without seeing how your emotion makes others feel?

Do you believe that people are often unkind to you?

Do you often think the worst of a situation??

Then **you may be a victim** of the tricky Unthinkable:

hmmph!

Grump Grumpaniny

Not to worry because there is help.

Superflex® has a couple strategies to defeat this character:

👍 **Think about** how the person treats you. Is he friendly or mean to you? If this person is friendly to you then it is likely that he is being nice to you.

👍 **Self talk:** "I am being negative. What could be a positive way to think about it?"

👍 _____

Appendix E: Additional Superflex™ and Unthinkable Handouts

Superflex®: A Superhero Social Thinking Curriculum
Think Social Publishing, Inc. ©2008 www.socialthinking.com

Bibliography and References

American Speech Language Hearing Association. (2005). *Evidence-based practice in communication disorders* . Position statement. Available online from http://www.asha.org.

Attwood, T. (2006). *The Complete Guide To Asperger Syndrome*. London: Jessica Kingsley Publishing.

Crooke, P.J., Hendrix, R.E., Rachman, J.Y. (2007). *Brief Report: Measuring the Effectiveness of Teaching Social Thinking to Children with Asperger's Syndrome (AS) and High Functioning Autism (HFA)*. Journal of Autism and Developmental Disorders, (38) 3.

Dobson, K. and D. Dozois. (2001). "Historical and Philosophical Bases of the Cognitive-Behavioral Therapies." In *K. Dobson Handbook of Cognitive Behavioral Therapies*. New York: The Guilford Press.

Dunn, K. and M. Curtis. (2004). *Incredible 5 Point Scale: Assisting Students with Autism Spectrum Disorders in Understanding Social Interactions and Controlling Their Emotional Responses*. Shawnee Mission, KS: Autism Asperger Publishing Company.

Gray, C. (1994). *Comic Strip Conversations*. Arlington, Tx: Future Horizons Publishers. http://www.FHautism.com

Gray, C. (2000). *The New Social Story Book*. Arlington, Tx: Future Horizons Publishers. http://www.thegraycenter.org

Linguisystems. (2004). *Guide to Evidence-Based Practice*. Linguisystems Inc.

Myles, B., M. Trautman, and R. Schelvan. (2006.) *The Hidden Curriculum: Practical Solutions for Understanding Unstated Rules in Social Situations*. Shawnee Mission, KS: Autism Asperger Publishing Company.

Winner, M. (2000). *Inside Out. What Makes a Person With Social Cognitive Deficits Tick*.

Winner, M. (2005). *Think Social! A Social Thinking Curriculum for School-Age Students*. San Jose, CA: Think Social Publishing Inc.

Winner, M. (2007). *Thinking About You Thinking About Me*. 2nd edition, San Jose, CA: Think Social Publishing Inc.

Winner, M. (2013). *Why Teach Social Thinking?*: Think Social Publishing, Inc.

110

The *Superflex* Series

Curriculum, illustrated storybooks, games, posters, and music CD

Hundreds of free articles are available on our website, including:

Superflex: Helping Kids Become Better Social Detectives, Thinkers, and Problem Solvers

10 DOs and DON'Ts for Teaching Superflex

Check out our eLearning Series on Superflex:

Superflex & Social Detective—A Mighty Duo! Best Teaching Practices

Four 90-minute modules expand your knowledge base... at your own pace...
in your own time... in your own place.

To learn more about Social Thinking and the Superflex curriculum series,
visit www.socialthinking.com

SocialThinking® has so much to offer!

OUR MISSION

At Social Thinking, our mission is to help people develop social competencies to better connect with others and experience deeper well-being. We create unique treatment frameworks and strategies to help individuals develop their social thinking and related social skills to meet their academic, personal and professional social goals. These goals often include sharing space effectively with others, learning to work as part of a team, and developing relationships of all kinds: with family, friends, classmates, co-workers, romantic partners, etc.

FREE ARTICLES & WEBINARS

100+ free educational articles and webinars about our treatment strategies

LIVESTREAM EVENTS, ON DEMAND COURSES & CUSTOM TRAINING

Live and recorded trainings for schools and organizations

PRODUCTS

Print and ebooks, games, decks, posters, music and more!

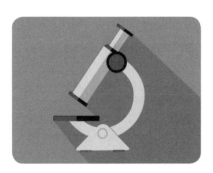

CLINICAL RESEARCH

Measuring the effectiveness of the Social Thinking® Methodology

TREATMENT: CHILDREN & ADULTS

Clinical treatment, assessments, school consultations, etc.

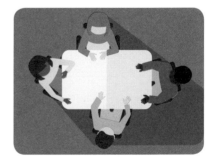

CLINICAL TRAINING PROGRAM

Three-day intensive training for professionals

www.socialthinking.com